WOMEN WHO DARED SERIES

Changing the Game

The Stories of Tennis Champions Alice Marble and Althea Gibson

Sue Davidson

Seal Press

Seattle

Seal Press
3131 Western Avenue, Suite 410
Seattle, Washington 98121
sealprss@scn.org

Library of Congress Cataloging-in-Publication Data
Davidson, Sue
Changing the game : the stories of tennis champions Alice Marble and Althea Gibson / Sue Davidson
1. Marble, Alice, 1913–1990. 2. Gibson, Althea, 1927– . 3. Women tennis players—United States—Biography. I. Title. II. Series.
GV994.A1D39   1997   796.342'092—dc21   96–51698
ISBN 1-878067-88-5

Printed in the United States of America
First printing, June 1997
10 9 8 7 6 5 4 3 2 1

Distributed to the trade by Publishers Group West
In Canada: Publishers Group West Canada, Toronto
In Europe and the U.K.: Airlift Book Company, London

Cover design by Design Lab
Cover photos: Upper, Alice Marble; Associated Press. Lower, Althea Gibson; Arthur Cole
Text design and composition by Rebecca Engrav

Photo acknowledgments
Pages xiii, 3, 4: all photos reprinted by permission of the International Tennis Hall of Fame; **page 91 (upper):** reprinted by permission of the International Tennis Hall of Fame; **page 91 (lower):** reprinted by permission of UPI/Corbis-Bettmann; **page 92:** reprinted by permission of Michael Cole Photography, © Arthur Cole.

To my first tutor in women's history, my daughter,
Erika Davidson Gottfried
and
To all the beloved sisterhood
of The Feminist Ex-Press

These stories, covering the years through 1991, are an account of major events in the lives of Alice Marble and Althea Gibson. Many quotations are from existing records of their lives and careers. Dialogue and details based on these records have also been added by the author.

Acknowledgments

In gathering material for this book and bringing it to its present form, I have had help from a number of sources.

It is a pleasure to thank those who read and commented on the manuscript in draft. Foremost among these—not only because his accessibility makes him easy to pester—is my husband, Alex Gottfried. By profession a political scientist, he is also a former intercollegiate basketball player, tennis player, and athletic coach. I have benefited from his ongoing and informed interest in sport, particularly in women tennis players and their history. I was also fortunate to have as a critic my longtime friend and sister-Texan Shirley Ann McRae, not only an active tennis player, but one who brought to her several readings her background as a teacher of English literature and grammar. Valuable suggestions were given to me by Lora Myers, a curriculum specialist currently supervising a project with teachers in the adult basic education program at the City University of New York. I am indebted to my friend Bettylou Valentine, Executive Director, Central Youth and Family Services, Seattle, for perceptive observations and questions and for ready consultation. Of particular importance to me also was discussion of the manuscript with Anna Birinyi, then in the ninth grade at Seattle's Garfield High School, and an all-around athlete currently participating in the school's interscholastic golf and swimming programs. Warm thanks, too, for the comments of my friend and former work colleague, Merle

Froschl, Co-director, Educational Equity Concepts, New York.

I am grateful for the assistance of my daughter, Erika D. Gottfried, Curator, non-print collections of the Robert F. Wagner Labor Archives, New York University, who located a special biographical file devoted to the career of Althea Gibson and reproduced its contents for my use. These materials, in the New Jersey Collection of the Newark, New Jersey Public Library, made it possible for me to fill in numerous details and to bring Ms. Gibson's story up to date. Other records, articles, and books I consulted are too numerous for listing here. Of central value to me were Alice Marble's first autobiography, *The Road to Wimbledon* (1946), and Althea Gibson's delightful early autobiography, *I Always Wanted to Be Somebody* (1958), as well as its autobiographical sequel, *So Much to Live For* (1968). All three books are, unfortunately, out of print. More current sources are *Courting Danger: Alice Marble*, by Alice Marble, with Dale Leatherman (1991), and *Althea Gibson, Tennis Champion*, by Tom Biracree (1990).

Astoundingly, after four books together, I have not worn out the patience of Faith Conlon, my Seal Press editor, with my endless arguments, lectures, and hair-splitting. Enduring them, she again applied herself to the main task of helping me craft a better book. I offer her my deepest thanks. Rebecca Engrav, also at Seal, has my thanks for a thorough and superior job of copyediting.

For any errors of fact or the interpretation of facts and events in the lives of my subjects, I take sole responsibility.

Contents

Undated photo. Alice Marble (left) and Althea Gibson (right) display the trophy awarded to winners of the Pacific Southwest Tennis Championships. Alice was the victor in this event in 1937 and 1939, Althea in 1956. Alice's powerful style was an early inspiration to the young Althea, who went on to create a smashing game of her own.

Introduction

Alice Marble (1913–1990) and Althea Gibson (1927–) are one-of-a-kind figures in the history of women's tennis. Each is recognized as having changed the game.

Alice Marble was the first woman to play tennis "like a man." Her powerful style influenced the way tennis has been played by all the female tournament players who followed her. Althea Gibson was the first to break the racial barrier in tennis. Her talent and bravery opened the door to participation by both black men and black women in world-class tennis.

Today almost all tennis fans—and even people who aren't—know who Althea Gibson is. Few of the same people under sixty-five have heard of Alice Marble. Yet, during her career, her name was familiar to millions. It isn't only the passage of time that has dimmed Alice Marble's fame. Rather, it's because her "power game" has now become so firmly established in women's tennis that it is taken for granted. Few fans today know of a time when Alice's game was not *the* game—or that Alice was the model.

Alice began to play tennis in the late 1920s, Althea about fifteen years later. Both fought their way into a sport which, at the time, earned players no money. Far from it, tennis was the game of those who already *had* money and social position. And Althea and Alice, although they lived at different levels of poverty, both came from families much too poor to support a daughter in a tennis career. The snobbishness of the tennis world alone would have been enough to scare off young women less proud and determined than Althea Gibson and Alice Marble.

There are other parallels in the characters of the two women. Each, in her own way, struck an important blow for civil rights at a crucial time. This was in an era when the struggle against racism—already well under way in boxing, football, and baseball—sent only a faint echo into the serene air of the nation's tennis clubs. When Alice and Althea each dared to defy the racism of the polite tennis world, their lives became directly linked.

The lives and careers of Althea Gibson and Alice Marble, alike, were full of ups and downs. On and off the court, each of these two magnificent athletes climbed to splendid heights, fell to painful depths, and then climbed up again—over and over. Their stubborn ability to survive would have made them remarkable women no matter what their walk of life. Their stories are so crowded with challenges, incident, and adventure that, as you read them, you may sometimes think that they couldn't really have happened, that they must be "made up."

But they are true.

Alice Marble

Alice Marble, undated photo. Alice's visored cap became her trademark after her recovery from a disasterous collapse brought on, in part, by sunstroke. Under the cap Alice always wore a cabbage leaf, as she'd been told farmworkers did for sunstroke protection.

Alice Marble jumping the net at the 1937 Wightman Cup match. Played between teams of the best women players of the United States and Britain, the matches held high prestige. Alice was chosen for the team in 1933, 1937, 1938, and 1939.

Alice Marble, undated photo. The picture was taken during World War II, probably as a promotion for the physical fitness council of the Office of Civilian Defense. Eager to join the struggle against Nazism, Alice accepted the post of co-chair of the council after unsuccessful efforts to join women's units of every branch of the U.S. military.

CHAPTER 1

An Early Taste of Fame and Sorrows

Like her mother, Alice wanted to be a singer. But that was only sometimes. More than anything else, she wanted to be a baseball player. She didn't become either. Instead, Alice Marble became one of the greatest players in the history of women's tennis.

Her mother, Jessie Wood, never got to be a singer, either. Instead, she became a nurse. Then she married and moved from San Francisco to northeastern California. There, she shared with her husband, Harry Marble, the work of running their farm. She and Harry had five children. Alice, born September 13, 1913, was the next to youngest.

In 1919, when Alice was six, her parents sold their farm. It was a successful farm, but Harry thought farm life was too hard on his wife. He took a job in San Francisco, bought a house, and the family moved in.

Jessie Marble was happy to be in San Francisco again, where her sister and brother lived. As for the Marble children, life in the big, ocean-side city of San Francisco was exciting after their simple life on the farm. For a while, everything went very well.

But soon there was sorrow and trouble for the Marble family. There was sorrow for many others, too, because the year 1919 brought a worldwide outbreak of flu. In the United States, many thousands caught the disease. Among them were Alice's brothers, Dan, George, and Tim, and her sister, Hazel. Harry Marble, their father, came down with pneumonia while recovering from an auto accident. On Christmas Eve, he died. "Christmas was never again a joyous time for me," Alice later said. "Not with the memory of my father's death."

Without Mr. Marble's earnings, the family suddenly became poor. Jessie's brother moved into the house, helping out with his earnings as a brakeman on a cable car. For a while, Jessie took a job cleaning office buildings. She rose at four in the morning, returning in time to feed her children and see them off to school. Then Dan, who was thirteen, left school to go to work. George, two years younger, followed after a couple of years.

It was a sad time, but the Marbles had always been a close, happy family. Jessie was brave and high-spirited. "We were so proud of Mother," Alice recalled. "All the neighborhood kids liked her. She was the only mother who ran races and played games with us. She beat everyone, too!"

The children were very fond of the uncle who came to live in their house. They called him "Uncle Woodie." He usually spent his day off with them, taking them to beautiful Golden Gate Park. It was Uncle Woodie who introduced Alice to her first love. That love wasn't a boy. It was baseball. By the time she was thirteen, baseball had made Alice a little bit famous.

Or, at least, for a while, in San Francisco.

■ ■ ■

It all started when Uncle Woodie taught Alice and her brothers to play baseball. Before long, they were playing on a team of neighborhood children, after school and on Saturdays. That stopped for Dan and George when they both went to work. Tim and Alice went on playing.

Uncle Woodie also often took the children to see Pacific Coast League baseball games at Recreation Park. It was thrilling to watch games played by their home team, the San Francisco Seals. After a while, Jessie let thirteen-year-old Alice and ten-year-old Tim go to the games by themselves. Alice earned the dime admission and the street-car fare by doing a few chores at the corner grocery store.

Alice and Tim always went to Recreation Park before the games started. They liked to play catch in the bleachers. In those surroundings, just behind the fenced-off baseball field, it was easy to pretend that they were real Coast League players.

Alice was good at catching the ball, and she had a powerful pitching arm. Tim was a good player, too, but he was younger and smaller than Alice. She held herself back sometimes, for fear of hurting him.

Tim had to hold himself back sometimes, too, to keep from laughing at the way Alice looked. She wore her blond hair cut very short and slicked back behind her ears. Sometimes she wore a skirt, but she also liked to wear britches. They looked funny to Tim. She wore George's old high-top tennis shoes. With that get-up, Tim thought, you could hardly tell that Alice was a girl.

One day when Alice and Tim were playing in the bleachers, a player in a uniform came over to the fence. He called:

"Say, boy, how'd you like to climb down and play with me?"

Alice saw that he was looking at her, not at Tim. She was a little angry that he had taken her for a boy. Still, she understood that the fence between them hid her skirt. Quickly, before he could change his mind, she leaped over the fence.

"I'm not a boy," she said, "but I'll play ball with you."

They began to play catch. As other players came onto the field, Alice thought they would tell her to leave. But they didn't. Then Alice's favorite Seals player, Lefty O'Doul, noticed her. He asked her to catch fly balls with him.

When it was almost time for the game to begin, O'Doul asked Alice her name. He invited her to come with him to the players' dugout. "This is Alice Marble," he said to the men gathered there. "She has a better arm than most of you guys!"

Alice found it hard to believe her eyes and ears. She was being welcomed by well-known players who were her heroes. "Hey, how about Alice coming out to warm up with us whenever we play?" one of them asked. The team's manager agreed that Alice should be their mascot.

The next afternoon, Alice's mother opened the door to a reporter from the *San Francisco Examiner*. He smiled and said, "If you're Mrs. Marble, you have a famous daughter." From his place in the dugout, the reporter had been watching Alice. He wanted to interview her and her mother.

The following morning, the *Examiner* carried a photo of Alice in action, wearing a baseball glove. The story beneath it had these headlines:

GIRL, AGED 13, PLAYS WITH P.C.L. STARS
Alice Marble Works Out Before Games At Recreation Park, Performs Like Veteran

Alice really did become famous among baseball fans. People talked to her at games and on the streetcar. They bought her and Tim popcorn and hot dogs and sodas. She had a wonderful time. When she wasn't practicing with the Seals, she was playing baseball in the neighborhood or on the girls' team at high school.

Her brother Dan was proud of her. Dan had become an outstanding athlete, playing handball at night. At nineteen, he was considered the best of all Northern California handball players. Alice watched him in matches, whenever he let her attend. Dan had become head of the family, now. He made more rules than Jessie did.

Alice still sang with her mother at home, and sometimes at church. But she didn't dream about being a singer anymore. She dreamed instead of becoming a baseball star.

When Alice was fifteen, her baseball dreams came to a sudden end. One day, Dan asked her to come upstairs to his and George's room. Reaching into the closet, he brought out a tennis racket.

"Who's that for?" Alice asked.

"I bought it for you," Dan said, "so you can learn tennis."

"Tennis!" Alice said. "I won't play that sissy game! What will the boys at school say? What will *the Seals* say!"

"But Allie, you've got to stop being a tomboy. You can't go on playing rough, boys' games. I want you to learn a ladylike sport. You can start tomorrow, on the courts at the park."

Tears came to Alice's eyes. She thought about all the fun she'd had, practicing with the Seals. She thought about the fame she'd earned. She was known as the "Little Queen of Swat." The crowd cheered when she was introduced, along with the Seals.

Dan said, "You'll like tennis, Allie. You'll be good at it."

Alice slammed out of the room. That night, she cried herself to sleep. But she knew she had to obey, once Dan made up his mind. Next day, her eyes still red, she went to the public tennis courts at Golden Gate Park. She had asked Mary, a girl at her school, to teach her how to play.

She and Mary played until dark. Mary taught her tennis rules—how to keep score, where to stand. She showed her how to grip the racket handle and how to serve the ball. Alice lost every game. And yet . . . she liked to swat the ball. She liked the "thwack" it made on her racket. She wanted to force that ball go where *she* wanted it to go.

And pretty soon, she liked tennis—a lot. In fact, she went to Golden Gate Park to play tennis every day after school, as well as on weekends. She took great pleasure in dressing for the tennis courts on weekends. She carefully washed and ironed her one tennis outfit, a long white pleated skirt and a simple white blouse. The britches she had once loved were long outgrown. In her first year of high school, she had grown six inches and had gained forty-five pounds. She was now on the chunky side, and she knew it. But when she put on her clean white tennis clothes, she felt almost like a movie star.

Alice and her friends often lingered on the courts until nearly dark. On one such evening, Alice was heading homeward, alone, on a tree-shadowed path in the park. She was humming a tune.

Suddenly, she felt herself grabbed from behind. Her voice was silenced by a hand clapped over her mouth. When she struggled to get free, she was roughly dragged into deeper darkness and thrown onto the ground. For an instant, the hand left her mouth. She tried to scream, but her attacker gripped his hands around her throat. Alice fainted.

When she came to, she was alone, and her clothing was torn. Sobbing, she sat up, and vomited from pain. She forced herself to her feet and dragged herself to the nearby home of her mother's sister. Aunt Josephine gently washed away the blood and dirt and phoned a physician. After that, she phoned Jessie. She told her Alice had a touch of flu and would stay at least overnight.

Some time after the doctor left, Alice and Aunt Josephine agreed that Jessie would not be told of the rape. The two of them explained Alice's bruises by saying she had fainted on Aunt Jo's stairs. When, three days later, Alice returned to school, she said she'd had the flu.

For a while, Alice felt terrified. In school, she wondered whether her attacker might be one of the faces passing her in the halls. She felt ashamed, too. Did her schoolmates know? Were they whispering about her behind her back? Could she ever regain her self-respect?

Above all, she felt that she could never have a real boyfriend, now that she wasn't a virgin. Nor did she want one. The contact she'd had with that male body was horrible. She wanted never to touch anyone intimately, or to be touched.

Aunt Jo urged Alice to put the whole thing behind her. "What's past doesn't matter a straw," she said. "Try to enjoy your life now, and look to the future, Alice darling."

Alice followed her Aunt Josephine's advice, in her own way. She excelled in sports, earning the admiration of schoolmates. They recognized that she was outstanding—not only in tennis, but in softball, basketball, and track. She could enjoy sports, take delight in the physical effort, take pride in herself, whatever the outcome of games. In sports, she could both lose herself and discover some nameless but precious part of herself. Especially, more and more, in tennis.

She played with all her heart.

CHAPTER 2

Both Sides of the Tracks

There were many social events during Alice's second year of high school. There were parties and dances, picnics and moonlight swims. Only—Alice didn't go.

It wasn't because she wasn't invited. Alice had plenty of friends. They included boys as well as girls, even though she didn't have a special boyfriend. Alice still liked boys—after all, her brothers were boys—but she hadn't changed her mind about not wanting a boyfriend since the rape.

Although Alice didn't dwell on the rape, she couldn't just forget about it, either. She was furious at the nameless man who had attacked her. At the same time, she went on being ashamed—as if, somehow, it had all been her fault.

It wasn't strange that Alice was so confused. In the 1920s, unlike today, rape was a forbidden topic. If anyone spoke about it at all, it was in whispers. Girls who were raped were seen by most people as "bad girls." People thought they must have done something to "ask for it"—worn the wrong clothes, been in the wrong place, at the wrong time. In most cases it was the girl or woman who was blamed rather than the man who raped her.

Alice was lucky to have her Aunt Jo. Aunt Jo didn't place any blame on Alice. She knew that Alice wasn't a "bad girl." Still, her aunt never quite put any of those opinions into words, and Alice, in turn, didn't talk freely about her feelings. It might have been much better if she had.

But at least Aunt Jo's silent respect helped Alice to be

friendly and enjoy a fairly normal social life. Her social life would have been even more enjoyable, if not for Dan's strictness. It was because of Dan that Alice didn't go to parties.

Sometimes she pleaded. "Just this once, Dan. It won't be very late, and I can—"

Dan cut her off. "You have a match to play tomorrow, Allie. Off to bed, now."

"Oh, all *right!*" Alice went storming up the stairs. "You never let me have any fun."

"Life isn't all fun," Dan yelled after her. "It's effort!"

Dan should know. He worked long, tiring hours at his job, laying down hardwood floors. Yet he also went on improving his handball game, at night and on weekends, at the YMCA. After a while, he was invited to join San Francisco's fashionable Olympic Club. Most of its members were as rich as Dan was poor. Dan had been offered membership because of his sports ability.

Dan was attractive, too, and he could be charming—when he wasn't angry. He got very angry during games, whenever anything went against him. He had a hot temper. So did Alice. Neither of them could bear to lose.

Mostly, though, Alice was winning. She had begun to win in junior tournaments at Golden Gate Park. The early hours, the strict discipline Dan demanded, paid off. By the time she was sixteen, she became champion of the park's Girls' Tennis Club.

"I was the only girl in the bunch who trained," she later said. "And it was Dan who did it."

But Dan could only do so much. Tennis, Alice found, cost money. The tennis courts at Golden Gate Park were free of charge, but the park didn't furnish tennis balls. They cost thirty-five cents each. To buy new ones regularly, Alice began to work at odd jobs, such as baby-sitting.

Besides that, the white tennis clothes Alice loved were no

longer a matter of choice. If you played in the Girls' Club tournaments, you were expected to wear a regular tennis outfit. When her first summer of tennis came, Alice found herself washing and ironing her one tennis outfit, over and over.

The Golden Gate Park tennis courts were open to the public. Therefore, they were crowded, and players had to take their turns. Like everyone else, Alice sometimes waited two or three hours for a chance to play. She didn't mind very much. She felt she learned a lot, just watching other players.

But Dan minded. He wanted Alice to be able to go to a private club, where she could get more practice. He soon bought her a junior membership at the California Tennis Club of San Francisco. Her membership cost Dan forty-five dollars of his hard-earned money.

It wasn't until then that Alice really began to see the difference between rich and poor. Saving up his earnings, Dan could buy Alice a membership in a private club. But he couldn't make its members play with her.

Alice knew many of the girls and boys who played tennis at Golden Gate Park. But she was a stranger at the California Tennis Club. The junior members went to different schools—often private ones—and had their own friends. They came from another world, a world where forty-five dollars wasn't a lot of money. The young people at the club could see that Alice was from "the wrong side of the tracks." They made her see it, too.

Alice was too shy to ask anyone for a game—and nobody invited her. Although Dan took Alice to the club week after week, she played no tennis there.

At that time, as the 1920s were ending, tennis was the sport of the rich. It had been that way since its start in England, in 1874. It remained more or less that way until well into the 1950s. "Lawn tennis," its real name, was an amateur sport, in which players could win silver cups—but no money. Yet tennis players needed money—not just for clothes and rackets, but often to pay a coach, as well as to join a tennis club. So the kind of people who belonged to private tennis clubs had to be fairly well-off. Besides that, they were expected to have good manners. Tennis was a sport for "ladies and gentlemen."

For that reason, the young people at the California Tennis Club weren't outright rude to Alice. They just ignored her.

Hurt and angry, Alice went back to Golden Gate Park. She loved the park, even though she knew its tennis courts weren't the best. The courts were so close together, players were always sending back balls that came from other courts. The asphalt was cracked, and some of the nets sagged. In short, the courts were run-down and shabby. Many who played there were, like Alice, from the "wrong" side of the tracks. That was true especially of the Asian-American players, who were usually kept out of "white" private clubs. In fact, even at the park, they were often snubbed by white players.

Alice had always been friendly with the Asian-American players. In turn, they were among the players who quickly welcomed her back. Some others, at first, made fun of her. They said that she'd gone "high hat" by joining a private club.

But soon all that was forgotten. Alice was liked and admired. With her baseball background, she was a strong player. When she played singles, she gave her opponent a tough game. In doubles, she was a good partner.

She continued to climb fast in the world of junior tennis. In the summer of 1930, she received an invitation from the Northern California Tennis Association, or NCTA. Would she be its representative in the Northwest and Canadian championships? The tour would take two and a half months. The association would pay seventy-five dollars toward her expenses, to be split with a chaperon chosen by the NCTA.

"Jeepers!" Alice yelled, when she got the news. She whirled around Dan and her mother in joyful circles. Slowly, she came to a stop. She saw Dan shaking his head.

"Not possible," Dan said. "You'll need more travel money than that. You'll need new clothes. I can't afford it now, Allie. You can go next year."

But Alice's heart was set on going. She took on more odd jobs. She sold her baseball glove and bat. In a few months, she had twenty extra dollars. Dan sighed. "Not enough, Allie."

Alice turned her head, to hide her tears. "I might as well give up," she thought. Then, one day toward the end of the school term, an envelope came for her in the mail. Inside were three twenty-dollar bills.

They didn't come from Dan or her mother. Alice never found out who sent them. "Whoever it was," she said in later years, "has my deepest thanks."

So, she set out, in June. She had two new rackets, given to her by a sporting goods company to advertise its products. Proud Uncle Woodie had given her ten dollars. Alice and Jessie had spent thirty dollars for Alice's new clothes. That left $97.50. It seemed like a fortune to sixteen-year-old Alice. She had no trouble keeping within her spending limits.

She did have trouble in her Canadian matches. In Vancouver, because of rain, play was delayed for three days. To make up the time, each player had to play extra matches daily. Alice was playing for the first time on clay courts—wet ones. As she slid around in her new shoes, blisters formed on her heels. When they became infected, a doctor advised her to quit.

But Alice refused to let California down. She went to her final match with the heels cut out of her shoes and rubber bands holding them on. She looked as funny as she used to look in her britches. It didn't matter to Alice. What mattered was that she went on—to win her first championship in a foreign country.

The next summer she became junior champion of Northern California. This meant that she could have the dearest wish of all young California tennis players: to go East, to play for the junior national championships.

The NCTA paid for travel and housing. But Alice was expected to have the clothes other young women had for "the nationals." Dan paid for ten changes of tennis outfits and three evening dresses. He had to work extra hours for the money.

Alice's doubles partner for the Eastern tournament was Bonnie Miller. Bonnie was the Southern California champion, from Los Angeles. Neither Alice nor Bonnie had experience on grass courts, since California courts were hard-surfaced. After a stop in New York, they went to practice at nearby Forest Hills, on the grass courts of the West Side Tennis Club. The courts were famous as the place where the U.S. national championships were played.

Alice didn't know Bonnie very well, but she was glad to be with her. Bonnie was easy and friendly—as nobody else at the club seemed to be. Even in her nice, new clothes, Alice felt shabby. "Wrong side of the tracks!" she thought. Then she squared her jaw. "I don't care which side of the tracks this is. If tennis champions play here, it's where *I* belong."

With this idea in mind, she went to New Jersey for the first match of the tour. She felt her old self-confidence, even a bit of conceit. She looked forward to smashing her opponent.

Her confidence lasted only a few minutes. Alice never knew where the ball was going to go, never mind if it was leaving her racket or coming toward her. Its bounce on grass was different from its bounce on asphalt—lower, and oddly angled. Her recent practice on grass courts with Bonnie did little good. Both had the same shortcomings—mainly, a Western grip on the racket handle which made it even harder to control the ball's bounce on grass and its flight path. Alice lost badly. She was almost shut out. The final score was 6–1, 6–0.

She and Bonnie didn't do any better in doubles. At their next two stops, they were beaten in their first match. By the time they returned to Forest Hills, Alice's spirit had sunk. She lost to her first opponent in less than half an hour. She crept back to the locker room, wanting to hide from everyone.

Yet she still had a chance at the main event. This was the U.S. National Junior Tennis Championships, to be played in Philadelphia. Because of her California record, she would play against the best players in the under-eighteen group. She watched these players in the early rounds of the singles. She told herself she *must* win here. "For Dan," she thought, "and Mother. And for the NCTA. They didn't pay my way here so I could *lose!*"

When her turn came, she fought hard. By using all her strength and skill, she struggled all the way to the final singles match. She faced Ruby Bishop, a top player—but one Alice had beaten easily in the past, in California. In Philadelphia, she did not beat Ruby. She won only five games in two sets. Before a huge crowd, Alice was badly beaten.

Alice shook hands at the net. Then she ran from the court as her tears started. Alone in her dressing room, she sobbed.

The door opened. In walked Mrs. Harrison Smith, the chairwoman of the tournament. She held out to Alice the runner-up prize, a silver medal. Alice's tears turned to rage. Grabbing the medal, she flung it across the room. "I don't want the damned thing!" she cried.

Mrs. Smith sat down on the bench next to Alice. After a moment, she said, "I know it's hard, Alice, but you have to learn to lose, as well as win. One is as important as the other."

Alice knew that Mrs. Smith was trying to be kind. "I'm sorry, Mrs. Smith," she said. She rose and picked up the medal.

But she was still angry when she and Bonnie began to play their doubles match a while later. She slammed balls any old way. They had lost the entire first set before Alice realized what she was doing. She was taking out her anger against Bonnie.

Bonnie hadn't made it to the singles finals. This was her chance, at least, to win at doubles. Bonnie didn't seem angry at Alice for letting her down. She went on playing her best—without Alice's help. Bonnie, Alice thought, was what Alice ought to be. A good sport!

She touched Bonnie on the shoulder. "Hey, Bonnie." She grinned. "Let's get 'em!"

Bonnie's face broke into a smile. "Okay!"

They began to fight as a team. The crowd saw the change. It began cheering for the Californians. Alice's heart lifted. She didn't even remember losing the singles match two hours before. She and Bonnie went on to win the doubles trophy.

People clustered around to congratulate them. Alice was struck by how warmly their opponents congratulated them. "Far from running off and crying," she later noted, "they smiled, and praised us to the reporters."

She hadn't yet learned the game she would need to learn. But she had learned something just as valuable. Back in San Francisco, when people asked about the match with Ruby, she told them: "She played too well for me. My strokes are okay for our hard California courts. But I need coaching to play on grass."

Philadelphia wasn't the last place where Alice lost her temper over tennis. Yet she had made a start at the gracious manner for which she later became well known. She'd made a start at learning to get along on both sides of the tracks.

CHAPTER 3

Enter: "Teach"

Dan Marble was sorry he'd never had a good education. He was eager for Alice to go to the University of California. In the 1930s, it charged no tuition fee for state residents. Alice's teachers also wanted her to attend. Although Alice spent a lot of time on sports, she'd earned good grades at school. Her teachers thought that she could probably pass the university entrance tests. And she did pass them easily.

One reason Alice did so well in school was that she was very good at memorizing. She had what many people call a "photographic memory." After she saw words or images once, she retained an exact picture of them in her mind's eye. She also knew how to make good use of the information in her head.

All the same, Alice put off going to the university. She wanted time to earn enough money to hire a coach and to go on practicing her tennis. At eighteen, while working part-time, she won the state singles championship. That got her into the Pacific Southwest Tennis Championships, and also again to Forest Hills—this time in the women's national matches. She came away from these events with more trophies. She was now the number one woman player in California, and seventh in the nation.

Yet she knew that she could not rise much further in tennis without coaching. She had strength, speed, balance, and hand-eye coordination, but she had never learned to play tennis properly. She'd learned through trial-and-error, hungrily studying the game of players who could afford coaching. Those were the players she had to compete with now, players from country club backgrounds. Her own background of poverty and public parks was an unusual one for a tournament player of the 1930s. But Alice wouldn't let that stop her. All she needed, she thought, was a coach. She wanted the best one in California, a woman named Eleanor Tennant.

That was who she got—even before she'd asked. Eleanor Tennant, who had watched Alice's matches, got in touch with her. She went to visit Alice and her family and offered to give Alice lessons. In exchange, Alice could work as her secretary and help with teaching her other students. This meant that Alice would have to travel down the coast frequently to stay in Southern California, where Eleanor Tennant had her home and offices.

"Teach" Tennant, as she was nicknamed, gave tennis lessons to many people who worked in the movies. Jessie Marble didn't like the idea of Alice's being around the "fast" Hollywood set. Besides, she didn't want Alice going off to live with a total stranger. Neither did Dan, but he could see that Alice was being offered a great chance to reach the top in tennis. Jessie thought of tennis as a nice, healthy activity, but not something to take very seriously.

Dan won Jessie over. He had plenty of help from Teach, because she made a good impression on Jessie. Teach charmed almost everyone she met. A tanned, slender woman in her mid-thirties, nearly Alice's height, she looked wholesome as well as handsome. Her short hair gleamed; her clothes were simple and smart. Her manner was polite and friendly. She was hard to resist.

In the end, Teach got what she wanted. She arranged a typing job for Alice with a San Francisco sporting goods company. Alice could work in the morning and be free to practice in the afternoon. The company would give Alice time off to travel to Southern California to visit Teach.

Alice had gotten what she wanted, too. Every dream she'd ever dreamed seemed possible now. "My coach!" she thought, scarcely breathing, as Teach moved gracefully out the door. "She's going to change my whole life!"

The thought was true in ways she could not foresee. For years to come, nearly every move Alice made was to be ruled by Eleanor Tennant. It was a state of affairs Alice wouldn't always find a blessing.

■ ■ ■

Before long, Alice joined Teach. She took a bus to the sea-side town of La Jolla, where Teach lived with her sister, Gwen. Years before, Teach had been married and divorced. She now supported Gwen, an older woman with a heart problem, who was immediately friendly to Alice.

After practicing with Alice a while on the courts, Teach said, "We're going to have to change your grip and shots." The next morning, right after breakfast, she said, "Let's jump into the car. There's someone I want you to practice with."

At a hilltop mansion overlooking the sea, Teach intro-duced Alice to Harold White—"Beese," as he was called. Tall and bald, he was a multimillionaire who sometimes taught top young players.

From the edge of his court, Beese watched Alice and Teach hit balls. After about ten minutes, he rose and spoke to Teach. "That," he said, "is just about the worst tennis I've ever seen."

Teach nodded. Alice's face went red. She was the seventh-ranking player in the nation! Who did they think *they* were? She flung her tennis racket the length of the court. "I'm certainly not going to take lessons from *him!*" she burst out.

Teach answered quietly. "If you want to go back to San

Francisco, fine. If not, pick up your racket."

Afer a moment, Alice went for her racket. Facing Beese White, she asked, "What do you want me to do?"

"First," he said, "we'll throw out everything you've learned, and start over."

Alice gritted her teeth. But in the weeks that followed, she tried to do as Beese said. She changed her strokes, starting by learning the Eastern grip. It was like a handshake on the racket and was more suitable for grass courts. It felt wrong to Alice, as did everything else she was learning. Often, she stalked away, ready to give up. And yet . . . the changes were working. Every day, she got more control into her shots.

She hated the lessons with Beese just the same. "Can't you coach me alone, Teach?" she begged. Teach answered: "You'll learn more from two of us."

Alice stuck to the new game, even though it cost her an important tournament the first season she used it. Then, in July 1933, she again won the women's singles title of California. Still nervous about the new game, she set out for the East.

She had tournaments to play in several places. She needed to win as many as possible to rise above her rank of number seven in the nation. Her ranking had grown even more important to her, because she hoped to be chosen for the Wightman Cup matches. The Wightman Cup matches were played between teams of U.S. women and British women. Only the best players were asked.

The first two tournaments saw her a winner. In the third one, she lost to a higher-ranked player. However, she and her partner beat the national doubles champions. In good spirits, she went to East Hampton, New York, for a three-day event. This one would determine whether or not she made the Wightman team.

When she reached the club at East Hampton, she was

stunned to find that she was on the program for both singles and doubles. She went to see Julian Myrick, committee chairman of the event. His greeting was cold, but she said politely: "Surely you don't expect me to play singles and doubles in three days, Mr. Myrick."

Myrick looked displeased. He said stiffly: "Mrs. Moody is doing you the honor of playing with her in the doubles."

Helen Wills Moody had been national women's champion seven times. The crowds thrilled to her game. Although the title had gone the previous year to Helen Jacobs, a superb player, Helen Jacobs had never beaten Mrs. Moody. Unlike the friendly Helen Jacobs, however, haughty Mrs. Moody was not popular with tennis players. They called her "Poker Face."

Alice said now: "Then suppose I play only in the doubles?" That way, she thought, she could save her strength for the Wightman Cup matches, which followed the three-day event by a week. Of course, she hadn't yet been chosen for those matches—and Julian Myrick was among those who did the choosing.

As if reading her mind, Myrick said: "To prove your worth, you'd better play the doubles *and* the singles." He turned away.

The other top players weren't being forced to "prove their worth" in this way. Unfair as it was, however, Alice gave in.

She had no problem making her way through the competition the first two days. But on the third day, she faced a killing schedule. She was to play in both the singles and doubles semifinal matches, starting at ten in the morning.

She fought hard and won the singles match, in scorching heat. Her head was throbbing when she heard: "Mrs. Moody is ready to play doubles!" Alice dashed off to change clothes, then ran back to the courts again. Helen Moody said coolly: "My back's bothering me, Alice. I don't want to strain it further."

Alice knew this meant that she would have to take all the overhead shots. Through three long, hard sets, she did double work, for a narrow victory. As Helen Moody smiled for the cameras, Alice, legs trembling, dragged herself off the court. She had one short hour before she had to play her singles final.

In the locker room, she saw that she had lost five pounds in three hours of play. Her joints were aching as she went out to face her opponent, former national champion Betty Nuthall. The temperature on the court had reached 104 degrees. Alice shook her head, to clear her vision.

Betty Nuthall came up to the net. "Are you okay, Alice?"

"I'm all right," Alice said. "Thank you, Betty."

Although Alice won the first set, Betty Nuthall had no trouble taking the match. Alice was exhausted. Now she had to change clothes, for the third time, to play the doubles final.

A few of the officials, and more than a few of the players, urged Alice to quit. "This is suicide!" she was told. She later learned that her well-wishers had also talked with Julian Myrick. He told them that the crowd had come to see Helen Moody play. That ended the matter, as far as he was concerned.

How Helen Moody felt about the matter, nobody knew. When she and Alice were defeated, she left the court without a word to Alice. People called to Alice from the stands, praising her for her effort. They applauded as she was helped off the court.

"A shame!" cried a fan. In nine hours, in broiling heat, Alice had played four matches totaling 11 sets, 108 games. She had lost fourteen pounds. That night, at the house where she was staying, she was unable to eat, but lay on the sofa. Getting up to join the other guests for coffee, she fainted. A physician said she had mild anemia and a sunstroke and should rest.

The New York sportswriters warmly praised Alice's "feat of strength." They also blasted Julian Myrick. Headlines screamed: "TENNIS ASSOCIATION FORCES ALICE MARBLE TO PLAY 108 GAMES." Teach blasted him, too, phoning from California. Myrick was furious at the bad publicity. But he didn't interfere in the choice of Alice for the Wightman Cup team.

Alice was delighted to make the team. She told herself that her weakness and dizziness would soon go away. But the day before the Wightman Cup contest started, the team doctor said she was still anemic. He forbade her to play in the singles. Then, on the final day, because she pleaded, he let her play in the doubles. Her strength gave out in the first set, however, and the match was lost. She felt terrible for letting down her teammates.

She also lost the singles in the quarterfinals of the national championships at Forest Hills. She had played well, but she had no staying power.

Even so, she would not admit that she was ill. At the end of her tour, she had risen from seventh to third place in the national rankings. She was a member of the U.S. team for the Wightman Cup. Teach, Beese, Dan, and her mother were proud.

As they welcomed her back to California, she thought that she would feel better, now that she'd left the hot, humid East.

But she didn't feel much better. On her return, she played in, and won, the Northern California championships—and then landed in bed with anemia again. Teach put her foot down. "No tennis for a while," she said. "I want you to *rest*. Eat your mother's cooking. Go to the doctor for your iron shots. I'll see you back in La Jolla in about two months."

When Alice returned to La Jolla, her health had improved. She again took up the rigid discipline of her life with

Teach. She took lessons, gave them to Teach's students, did office work. Bedtime was early. At age twenty, she had no friends and no social life with anyone her own age in La Jolla.

Yet, Alice thought, nobody was luckier than she. It wasn't only the tennis training, although that was the most important factor. But also, her everyday life was a little like going to the movies. Tennis was a big thing, in those days, among movie people—and they flocked to Teach for lessons. Alice, a movie fan, never tired of seeing the "stars twinkling" on the courts.

She soon met many more famous people. One day, Teach told her to pack a suitcase. "We're going to visit Hearst Castle," she said. "We'll spend a month giving lessons there."

Alice gulped. She had, of course, heard of William Randolph Hearst, publisher of a giant chain of newspapers. She had also heard of the fabulous castle where he lived with movie star Marion Davies. The castle, high on a hilltop in San Simeon, California, was surrounded by forty thousand acres of land. It was a gathering place for celebrities. Over the years, Alice was to meet too many to count—such immortal stars as Charlie Chaplin, Marlene Dietrich, Jean Harlow, and Bing Crosby. She met directors, painters, journalists, and authors.

She became a favorite of Mr. Hearst and Miss Davies. When the great Irish playwright George Bernard Shaw visited, they chose Alice to be his dinner partner. He and Alice talked far into the evening. Afterward, Teach asked: "What on earth did you talk about?" "About him," said Alice. "I wrote a paper on his plays as part of my college entrance exams. I remember every play."

Teach grinned. "Your photographic memory comes in handy!"

To Alice's surprise, the guests at Hearst Castle were often

as interested in meeting her as she was in meeting them. Many were tennis fans. They liked Alice's honesty and simple friendliness.

Sometimes, at parties, guests were asked to entertain. Alice responded one night by singing a song. Her talent was noted, and after that, she was often asked to sing—among guests whose performing talents were known by millions. When they applauded, Alice felt she must be dreaming.

Among the guests who admired Alice was the journalist Arthur Brisbane. His column appeared in all the Hearst newspapers around the country. He wrote:

> **What a girl Alice Marble is, with everything the Venus de Milo has, plus two muscular, bare, sunburned arms marvelously efficient. Her legs are like two columns of polished mahogony, bare to the knees, her figure perfect. . . . She should marry . . . and be the perfect mother with twelve children, not merely the world's best tennis player, which she probably will be.**

It was typical of the times that Brisbane hoped Alice would marry and have twelve children. That seemed a goal as desirable for her as "merely" becoming the world's best tennis player—as unlikely as that would be, with twelve children.

Teach knew better. She had to struggle just to support herself and her sister and to pay expenses to further Alice's career. But she didn't object to the publicity for her young champion.

It was Alice's mother who objected. She was shocked to think that remarks on Alice's body were being read all over the nation. She wrote to say that Alice must come home at once.

As usual, Teach smoothed out everything. Alice stayed.

CHAPTER 4

Skyrocket

The white-haired fortune-teller gripped Alice's hands. Her voice rose above the dance music in New York's famous Waldorf-Astoria ballroom. Staring at Alice, she said: "You will rise like a skyrocket and then fall to the ground."

A shiver ran through Alice. She pulled her hands loose, stood, and turned to her partner, who nimbly danced her away.

Swaying to the music, Alice tried to recapture the glad mood of the farewell party for the Wightman Cup Players. Paris! They were going to Paris and then London! The Wightman Cup matches were played between teams chosen from the best U.S. women players and the best British players. Usually the American team traveled only to England, to play the British. This year, 1934, the U.S. team would first play a series of matches in France.

It was like a fairy tale, Alice thought. Tomorrow, she would board a ship for the first time and sail across the Atlantic. She only wished that Teach were going, to help keep up her spirits. Since her ordeal at the East Hampton tournament, her strength still seemed to come and go. That was why the fortune-teller's words had startled her. But if Teach took two months away from teaching, there would be no income to support either of them. So, Alice just had to make the best of it.

The next morning a crowd gathered to cheer the members of the team as they boarded the ship. Photographers called, "Look here, Miss Marble, here!" She laughed and waved to them.

In the excitement of the send-off and on the voyage that followed, Alice's fears faded. By the time the ship docked at Le Havre, France, she felt only a little tired. She was cheered by the sight of Helen Jacobs, who met the team's train in Paris. All the team liked Helen, their captain and number one player.

Helen, however, wasn't cheered by the sight of Alice at team practice the next day. They were at the Stade Roland Garros, where the matches were to be played. The stadium has high walls at both ends, so that little air gets to the courts. Although it was only May, it was hot. After Helen quickly beat Alice two sets in a row, she said, "I'm worried, Alice. You look drained."

She sent Alice to the team's physician, who had her blood tested. "You're slightly anemic, but you can play," he told her.

Alice breathed a sigh of relief. Later, she thought it was her last clear breath of the entire trip. She played her first match of the series against Sylvia Henrotin, France's number two player. The day was sweltering. Alice's racket kept slipping in her hand. Like most of the French players, Sylvia didn't look very athletic—but she ran Alice all over the court.

Alice couldn't understand the score being called out in French. She was less interested in the score than in trying to get her breath. Her chest hurt. She lunged forward to return Sylvia's serve. She felt herself stumbling, falling, falling . . .

She woke to find herself in a hospital bed. She was told that she had fainted, probably from sunstroke. The French physician said her chest pain was caused by pleurisy, an illness coming from her lungs. Therefore she could not go to England with the team. Alice wept, Helen Jacobs's arms around her.

Helen arranged for the American Embassy to get Alice

aboard a ship whenever she was released from the hospital. She had cabled Teach, who would meet Alice in New York.

The day after Helen and the team left for London, the physician gave Alice his final report. "My dear girl, I'm very sorry. I have bad news for you. You have tuberculosis."

Unbelieving, Alice stared at him. Tuberculosis! It was a dread disease, sapping strength, fatal if untreated. He added soberly: "You will never be strong enough to play tennis again."

Alice said nothing, but turned her face to the wall. That night she prayed to die. If she couldn't play tennis, what was there for her? Her life was over, just when it had barely begun.

She went on praying to die each day, lying in her hospital bed. She knew that her mother—who wrote daily—would be grieved by this wicked misuse of prayer. Her mother! And Dan! After all they'd done for her, she'd be nothing but a useless burden to them now. Where would the money come from, to pay for the expenses of her illness? And with her career smashed, how could she ever repay Teach? Much better to die.

Six weeks later, in a wheelchair, Alice was trundled off a ship to Teach. Alice saw tears in Teach's eyes as she bent down to kiss Alice's cheek. At just that moment, the secretary of the tennis association bustled up to them. "I'm here," he said, "to take you to the offices of the U.S. Lawn Tennis Association. Miss Marble, you must make an accounting to us of your expenses."

Teach glared at him. "Why—you stupid damn fool! Can't you see this girl is ill?" She pushed Alice toward a waiting taxi.

A few days later, at the New York hotel to which Teach took Alice, Teach had a ferocious shouting match with

Julian Myrick. Teach insisted that Myrick had ruined Alice's health by forcing her to play too many matches at East Hampton. She said that the tennis association must help pay all future medical expenses. "Out of the question!" said Myrick. "We paid her passage and the hospital—and she never played one match. And since she'll never play tennis again, we won't get it back from gate receipts."

At last, Teach gave up, screaming, "Get the hell out!"

Alice thought she could not feel more miserable—but when she got home, to San Francisco, she did. She was immediately put to bed, where she spent long, wretched days. Seeing her pale face and hollow eyes, Dan struggled for something to say. Alice's divorced sister, Hazel, left early for work. At night she did household chores. That was because Jessie was no longer well. Jessie cooked Alice's meals, carrying trays up the long flight of stairs. Her every laboring footfall gave Alice pain.

Teach drove up from Los Angeles, where she and Gwen now lived. She brought in a specialist who said that Alice could improve in a warmer climate. Teach offered to take her back to Los Angeles. Dan didn't like it, and Jessie was hurt, saying: "She can get all the care she needs right here." Alice said, "But, Mom, it's too much for you. Please, it's best." The day Alice left, Jessie kissed her cheek, then wordlessly walked away.

Teach didn't drive to Los Angeles but to Monrovia, twenty-five miles from there. She took Alice to Pottinger's Sanatorium, a private hospital for the treatment of tuberculosis patients. "You'll get six weeks of total rest, under a doctor's care," Teach cried enthusiastically, waving her arm at a circle of neat cottages sitting on green lawns, "in this lovely, quiet place!"

But Alice hated the sanatorium at first sight. She also learned to hate Dr. Pottinger. At her weekly checkups, he never gave her any solid information. Alice would ask, "Am I getting well? Are my lungs clearing? Is my blood count up?" Dr. Pottinger only smiled and said, "You're getting on nicely."

The day the six weeks ended, Alice was packed and ready to leave. Dr. Pottinger followed Teach into Alice's room. "You'll need another six weeks of rest," he told Alice.

Alice didn't see how she could bear six more weeks lying in bed. Except to go to the bathroom, she wasn't allowed to get up. When the second six weeks had dragged by, she tried dressing to leave, but her clothes didn't fit. The absence of exercise, the rich diet, had added inches to her figure. She hadn't combed her hair or packed when Pottinger said, "Six more weeks."

Not long before her twenty-first birthday, a nurse brought Alice a letter. It said:

Dear Alice,

You don't know me, but your tennis teacher is also my teacher, and she has told me all about you. Once I thought I had a great career in front of me, just like you thought you had. Then one day I was in a terrible automobile accident. For six months I lay on a hospital bed, just like you are today. Doctors told me I was through, but then I began to think I had nothing to lose by fighting, so I began to fight. Well, I proved the doctors wrong. I made my career come true, just as you can—if you'll fight.

The letter was signed "Carole Lombard." Alice read it again and again. Carole Lombard, the movie star—writing to her, caring about her! At this time, the country's main entertainment was the movies, and Carole Lombard was adored by millions. Teach told Alice that Carole's face had been horribly cut up in the auto accident. But Carole had refused to accept the verdict of the doctors who said her career was over. She'd lived through months of painful surgeries before her face—her fortune—was at last restored. She'd found the inner strength to fight back.

A few months later when Teach visited, Alice abruptly announced: "I have to leave this place." Teach said, "I've just seen the doctor. He promised you might leave in one month."

Alice shook her head. She'd been told that before—and she'd been here for eight months. Meanwhile, Teach, working double time, was being milked for money. "I refuse to believe him, or even you," Alice said. "I'll die in this place if I stay." Saying it, she realized she no longer wanted to die.

Teach took a quick breath. Then she said quietly, "Can you make it to the car?" Alice nodded. Leaning on Teach, she moved slowly into the night air. At the car, she began to black out, but Teach caught her in her arms. Opening the door, she shoved her inside, then raced around and leaped into the driver's seat.

When they reached the highway, Teach shouted, "Getaway!" They began to giggle. "Bang, bang, bang!" Alice cried.

"I knew then," Alice remembered, "that there were two *me's*—the strong one and the weak one. I'd left the weak one behind me, in the sanatorium. I knew then that I could get through."

■ ■ ■

With Teach's help, Alice worked out a plan to get back her strength. It began with walking a block each day, then two, until she could walk three miles. After that, she added jump rope and swimming. Teach put her on a diet, too. During her months in the sanatorium, she had gained nearly fifty pounds.

At first it was "sheer agony," Alice said, to stick to this routine. Often, there didn't seem to be much point to it. "What can I *do* with my life?" she asked herself. "I can't let Teach go on and on supporting me. I'm no use to her anymore."

Of course, that wasn't quite true, since Alice had taken up Teach's office work again. Yet she knew she was no longer of any money-making use to Teach. The only way to repay Teach was by helping to preserve and build her fame as a coach. Tennis remained an "amateur" sport; no money went to champions—only the fame that came with being a star. Alice's stardom was behind her. Why, she wondered, did Teach put up with her?

Teach explained, "I believe in you." That was what Carole Lombard said, too. Alice and Carole had come to know each other better and better after Alice left the sanatorium, developing a fond, happy friendship almost from their first meeting. Alice found it hard to share Carole's and Teach's belief in her. But their belief and Jessie's daily letter from San Francisco made it possible for her to go on.

About four months after the "getaway" from the sanatorium, when Teach still hadn't settled on a suitable physician for Alice, Carole urged that they try a Los Angeles specialist, Dr. Commons. Alice liked him immediately. Unlike Dr. Pottinger, he didn't treat her like a child. When he had examined her and her x-rays, he asked: "Tell me, what do you want most in the world?"

"To get well and play tennis again."

"Well," Dr. Commons said, "I think you can do that. You've had pleurisy in the past. Your lungs are pretty scarred. But you do not have tuberculosis. Maybe you never had it."

Tears came to Alice's eyes. Dr. Commons went on, "You're anemic, but you can overcome that. If you follow my instructions, there's no reason you can't play tennis again." Dr. Commons gave her a new diet: vegetables and fruits only. When her blood count went up to seventy-five and she'd lost twenty pounds, he said, she might begin her tennis practice.

With raised hopes, Alice threw herself into her daily routine. She enjoyed the exercises that had been a chore. She didn't enjoy passing up sweets and second helpings. Her rewards came in seeing her weight go down and her blood count go up.

Best of all, training with Teach, her skills slowly returned. At the end of a year, she played in the Racquet Club tournament at Palm Springs, in very hot weather. Under her cap she wore a cabbage leaf, as Dr. Commons told her farmworkers did to cool their heads and avoid sunstroke. She faced the player who'd replaced her as number three in the nation during her illness. She won 6–2, 6–2.

Now Dr. Commons said she might play in the state tournament at Berkeley, in Northern California. She went beforehand to visit her family. It was a happy reunion, but Alice was troubled by how thin her mother was. She didn't know that Jessie had cancer, for Jessie had sworn the family to secrecy. Except for being thin, Jessie seemed the same. She fussed over Alice's health and repeated her old concerns about Alice's "fast" Hollywood friends.

Alice's Hollywood friends weren't "fast"—or, Alice thought, not what most people saw as fast. They smoked, they drank at parties—but so did Dan! That didn't influence Alice's habits. However, if her mother ever learned that Teach was a lesbian, that might cause her genuine shock. On the other hand, Jessie probably didn't know what a lesbian was. Alice hadn't known, herself, when someone first told her about Teach. After her first amazement, Alice decided it didn't matter. Teach wasn't her lover—more like a big sister or an older friend. Anyway—whose business was it?

When Alice returned to play in Northern California, sports reporters in the area took notice of the event. There was praise for her brave fight against illness and her comeback. But there was also criticism of Alice's style of play.

Although Alice's style caused a lot of comment now, it had made sports reporters uneasy before this tournament. For Alice had brought something entirely new to women's tennis. As one writer put it, she was "the girl who played the same game as the fellas."

A typical headline of the period read, "MARBLE'S PLAYING A MAN'S GAME." What did that mean, and what was new about it?

First, with her baseball background, Alice Marble hit with a strength and power more commonly seen in men. Beyond that, she played what is called a "serve and volley" game. This meant that when the ball returned to her, she did not wait for it to bounce, but moved right in to smack it. This "man's" game often had to be played close to the net. Women played closer to the back of the court, near the baseline, from which the ball is served. Even from the baseline, Alice's strokes were fast and hard, her whole game an attack.

After Alice's fame grew, many women players began to take up her aggressive game. Women's tennis came to resemble more closely the game played by men. Among modern female stars, only Martina Navratilova has consistently played Alice's "serve and volley" game. But Navratilova, Steffi Graf, Monica Seles, and others play with enormous power. Most female champions are now also taller, larger, and stronger than those of Alice's day.

Still further back, in the late 1800s when tennis began, few women players were as strong as Alice. They were also hampered by their clothes—long skirts, tight waists, stockings. Clothing was more sensible by Alice's time. However, even after shorts were in fashion, Alice was the first to wear them in a tennis tournament—upsetting many spectators.

Some members of the overflowing crowd at the Berkeley finals in 1936 were upset with Alice, too. This time, it was because of the rivalry between Northern and Southern California tennis fans. The northern fans felt that Alice had "defected" by following Teach south, and they showed their coolness. Other than Alice's family, Teach, and Carole, almost everyone cheered Alice's San Francisco opponent.

Alice felt hurt. After all, she thought, San Francisco was her home town, too! It was hard to play with the crowd against her. But she had so much at stake that, within a few minutes, she forgot the crowd. Although her opponent was outstanding, Alice won—in the amazing time of only half an hour!

Teach and Carole went wild, and so did the crowd. Alice and her partner also won the doubles title. Now she began to hope Dr. Commons would say she could go East this very season.

She continued building her health and her game. She now practiced only with men, as Teach and Beese wished. Soon Dr. Commons said she might play in the Southern California championships. She won—and was California's number one again.

When Dr. Commons examined her next, he made up his mind about the Eastern trip. "You're strong and well enough to go," he said. Alice cried, "Thank you!" and threw her arms around him. With her new title, she would represent Southern California in all the Eastern tournaments and "the big one"—the national championships at Forest Hills.

Teach had vowed that, this time, Alice was not to go without her. She was afraid something terrible might happen again. On June 20, 1936, the two of them started east in Teach's car.

Along the way, to earn money for the trip, Teach did promotion for a sporting goods company. She also gave tennis clinics—classes presented to as many as 5000 people. At night, she dictated articles for the Hearst papers. Alice typed them, and they appeared in the next day's sports pages. With this routine, they traveled from one major city to the next.

Their last stop before New York was at a farmhouse in Ohio. It was the home of former tennis champion Mary K. Brown. "Brownie" was a gentle, kind person, who was to become Alice's lifelong friend. Their friendship began on Brownie's tennis court, where she and Teach coached Alice daily for the coming tournaments.

Besides Brownie's coaching talents, she had strength of character, good sense, and sound judgment. Alice began to see those qualities very soon, the day an unexpected telegram arrived.

CHAPTER 5

Fame

The telegram stated that the U.S. Lawn Tennis Association refused Alice's entry to *all* the Eastern tournaments! The reason given was that she wasn't well, and the USLTA didn't want to be responsible if she collapsed again.

"But—Dr. Commons sent them a report verifying my health!"

Teach exclaimed, "It's that damned Myrick!" She dashed to the hall phone, but Brownie followed her. "No, please, Eleanor. It won't help if you and Myrick get at each other's throats."

Brownie offered to go with them to New York and see what she could do. Talking with USLTA officials there, she found that the decision might be changed if Alice proved her fitness in practice matches—with men only. Teach swore. "Myrick! He still wants to kill her!" But Alice grasped her arm and cried, "Let me do it! I can do it." She looked over at Brownie, who said quietly:

"You'll be right *there*, Eleanor. If it's too much for Alice, you can stop it." At last, Teach sighed. "Well. Okay."

Alice played a series of men, for four straight days, in hot sun. She played well and didn't tire. The committee of judges—even Myrick—gave its okay.

Delighted, she began touring the tournaments—and won three in a row. But at Rye, New York, playing France's Sylvia Henrotin again, her Paris breakdown haunted her mind. She played poorly, and lost. After that, at the Essex Country Club,

41

she faced her friend Helen Jacobs. Like Alice, Helen was to play this season's national championships, which she'd won four times in the past.

The game between Helen and Alice was close, but in the end Helen won. Alice didn't feel bad. Helen was a great champion, with a brilliant record behind her. Alice felt she'd played well against the champion. She went to Forest Hills in good spirits.

Her mood became uncertain there. A number of club members asked about her health. One said, "Is it wise for you to play in this heat?" Alice thought: "Is it? Am I really well?" Then she realized she'd been playing in the heat for weeks. She laughed, tucked her cabbage leaf in place, and went out to the courts.

In a large stadium, there are many courts. The center court is where the most important matches are played. Alice was thrilled to be on the center court at Forest Hills. She won match after match—and found herself in the finals against Helen.

No one, including Teach and Brownie, really expected Alice to beat Helen. Neither did Alice. Like the others, she only hoped she'd make a good showing in that match of September 12, 1936. Warming up and getting dressed, she tried to stay calm.

From the loudspeaker the announcement blared: "This match will be between Miss Helen Jacobs, four times national champion and winner of the Wimbledon championship, and Miss Alice Marble of San Francisco." Alice and Helen strode onto the court.

Across the net, stocky, wide-shouldered, and composed, Helen looked unbeatable. Alice was so nervous that, at first, she could only play like a machine. That at least kept the first set close. Alice was relieved that Helen won it by no more than two games, 6–4. Gaining confidence, Alice took the second set—easily, to her surprise.

The stands buzzed with excitement as Alice and Helen went to their dressing rooms for the ten-minute break. Teach helped Alice take off her sweat-soaked clothes. Teach's hands were shaking. She poured tea for Alice, saying, "Hit to her forehand and run to the net. Make her hurry her shots." Alice nodded, hardly listening. She and Teach had already taken apart Helen's game and planned the strategy Alice should use, many times.

Alice and Helen resumed their play. The crowd was with Alice, as the underdog. But after she'd won the first four games rapidly, the cheering shifted to the defending champion, Helen. Helen took two games, Alice the next. Alice led five games to two.

After the players changed courts, they were soon at a tie. Then Alice pulled ahead until the score was 40–15, her favor. This was "match point," meaning that if Alice won the next point, the match was hers. She hesitated, trying to choose her best tactic. Deciding, she served a sizzler, then raced to the net.

Helen returned the ball high over Alice's head and behind her. Alice whirled, ran back, reached up and caught the ball with her racket. She smashed the ball hard into the backcourt.

Screams and applause told her that her return was within bounds. She heard the umpire call:

"Game, set, and match, Miss Marble, 4–6, 6–3, 6–2."

She threw her racket into the air and ran to meet Helen. Smiling, Helen shook her hand. "Well played, Alice."

She'd done it. With the help of those who'd had belief in her, she'd fought her way back and up, from illness and despair.

And now she was champion of the United States.

■ ■ ■

Stars in almost any sport get a lot of public attention. That was especially true in the United States in 1936, when Alice won the national tennis championship. At that time the country was in the midst of the Great Depression. Hit by hard times, millions of Americans had lives that offered few pleasures. Many found pleasure in glimpses of the lives led by public figures who seemed glamorous and exciting—like movie stars and sports champions. Even if ordinary people couldn't experience the life of a star, the star could be brought closer through newspaper and magazine stories, newsreels, radio, and public appearances.

Thus, when Alice won the national tennis championship, the whole world seemed interested in her overnight. She was everybody's darling—even Julian Myrick's. He boasted about Alice as if he'd long been her admirer, not her foe. Teach took immense satisfaction in Myrick's about-face. She also took immense satisfaction in sharing the spotlight with Alice. She felt that she'd earned her share of it—and so did Alice. Half the fun of victory, for Alice, was Teach's pride and pleasure.

It wasn't hard for the public to admire Alice. With her golden hair and glowing skin, she was the "Golden Girl" of sunny California. Yet, even with her air of glamour, she was a pattern of "the simple, clean-cut, all-American girl." She wasn't a smoker or a drinker. She didn't come from a snooty country club background. She'd worked her way up from the public parks. She gave hope to young athletes without money or connections. Ordinary folk took pride in her triumph over poverty and illness. Open, friendly, smiling, Alice Marble was "just like you and me."

Coming home to San Francisco, Alice was met at the train station by the mayor. In an open car full of flowers, he rode with Alice and Teach at the head of a parade—led by her brother Dan, now in the motorcycle police. The rest of her family rode in an open car behind her. In the crowd lining the streets were tennis friends and schoolmates. Alice waved, shouting with delight.

Nearer home, all the neighbors turned out. There were

hugs, tears, and more shouts. Then, at the curb in front of the Marble home, Alice spotted a shining green Chevrolet. It was a gift from William Randolph Hearst and Marion Davies. Tied to the steering wheel was their note: "To the winner go the spoils."

The gleaming new car with its note from rich, famous people said a lot about the young woman who now, her arm around her mother's waist, entered the slightly shabby white house. For four years, Alice had moved among the wealthy. Meanwhile, she didn't have a dime of her own. She wasn't paid a fee for appearing in tournaments, as tennis players are today. The prize for winning wasn't cash—it was a trophy. She couldn't hold a regular job because, like all top players, she had to train and travel constantly. And, unlike today's players, she couldn't take pay for endorsing products. The USLTA didn't allow it: such practices might cheapen "the sport of ladies and gentlemen."

The result of all this was that tennis players either had to have well-to-do families or rich patrons to support them. Alice had Teach—but Teach wasn't rich.

Alice became more painfully aware of her own family's financial state when she came home in 1936. By then, Jessie could no longer hide her illness. She confessed to Alice that she had cancer. On top of Alice's grief, she realized that the whole burden of medical bills was on her brothers and sisters. She needed a *paying* job, to help out. Tear-choked, she told Jessie, "I'm staying here with you."

Jessie put her arms around Alice. "Now you're well, do you think you'd make me happy staying here? I want you to go *on*."

Nothing Alice said could make Jessie change her mind. So Alice returned to Los Angeles some weeks later, her heart heavy.

It helped that she had so much to do. She received stacks of fan letters daily. Those had to be answered, as well as

Teach's correspondence. As in New York, there were also public appearances. She spoke at the ceremony when the Golden Gate Bridge was opened in San Franciso and at many other gatherings.

Alice was busy, above all, working on her game. Hour after hour, Teach drove her with no mercy. She was preparing Alice for the 1937 All-England Championships, at Wimbledon. This international event was the world's most important competition. After Wimbledon, Alice would return to the United States, to play the East Coast tournaments and defend her new title at Forest Hills.

But in the spring, when she and Teach boarded their ship, Alice didn't want to think that far ahead. Twenty-three years old and feeling marvelously fit, she wanted to live in the moment and enjoy herself.

There were strict limits, however, to what Teach let Alice enjoy. Alice could have danced until dawn, but Teach made sure she was in bed by ten. (It was Teach—high-spirited, elegant, her hair now a cap of shining silver—who partied half the night.) Teach also made it clear that there were to be no shipboard romances for her young star. "Love and tennis don't mix," Teach liked to say.

"Oh, Lord," Carole had said to Alice a few months back, when the two of them were gossiping and joking, "you can disobey Teach once in a while!" She rolled her eyes mischievously. But Alice had become serious, shaking her head. "Oh, no," she said. "I owe Teach almost everything. I want her to be proud of me."

And Teach *was* proud. In England, losing her usual caution, she boasted to the flocks of reporters who trailed them that Alice's Wimbledon victory was a sure thing. "Nothing can stop Alice," Teach said. "She's the best woman player in the world."

At Wimbledon, Alice slipped away from Teach and fans to

stand alone before the famed arch at the entrance to the center court. The words inscribed there, by the English writer Rudyard Kipling, were familiar to her, as they were to many players:

> *If you can meet with Triumph and Disaster*
> *And treat those two imposters just the same.*

Could she? Alice asked herself. Could Teach? They'd worked so hard and been through so much together—more misfortunes than most players ever face. They'd come so far, almost to the top. What waited for them now? Would it be triumph or disaster?

As things turned out, that summer of 1937, it was disaster. Alice reached the semifinals, beating Denmark's Hilda Sperling, fourth-leading player in the world. But in the semifinals, Polish champion Jadwiga (JaJa) Jedrzejowski defeated Alice.

Alice was *out*? Yes, out of the Wimbledon singles—before even reaching the finals! Alice and Teach were stunned.

The British reporters to whom Teach had bragged could snicker at her now. Teach pulled herself together to face them, while Alice wept in the dressing room she shared with JaJa. In her broken English, JaJa tried to comfort her. "You play so *good*, Alice! It is only the luck. This time I am lucky one."

Alice knew that in fifty-three years, only four women had won the Wimbledon singles in their first attempt. But she made no such excuses to the waiting reporters. Tears wiped away, she said: "JaJa played beautifully. She was just too good for me."

Teach didn't berate herself for her overconfidence. She stopped Alice's moaning, too. "You forget," she said, "that you still have the doubles to play. You can still bag a trophy."

Yes, she still had the doubles—and she determined to win. Her partner was another Californian, red-haired Donald

Budge. He'd already won the men's singles and doubles. If he now also won the mixed doubles, in which a male and female couple face another "mixed" couple, he'd become the number one male player in the world. He and Alice did win, 6–4, 6–1.

"It was like playing two men!" the breathless losers said to the reporters. With Don's arm around her shoulder, the former Little Queen of Swat grinned in tomboy glee.

With her English partner, Kay Stammers, Alice lost in the early rounds of the women's doubles, but her high spirits weren't dampened. She felt restored by the mixed doubles victory, happy that she had, at least, one trophy to show for Wimbledon. Next year, she'd do better there. Her life in tennis, she thought, as she and Teach sailed homeward to New York, was by no means over.

But that summer she began to fear that perhaps it *was* over. At first she felt fit and confident, beginning the Eastern tournaments. It didn't bother her to be facing JaJa again, this time at Seabright. JaJa was a talented player, but Alice agreed with the press that Alice Marble was a better one. So she was a little surprised when JaJa defeated her at Seabright. When she lost again, at both Rye and Westchester, Alice began to unravel.

At Forest Hills, where she was to defend her title, she didn't reach even the semifinals. It was JaJa who played in the final match. There, at last, she lost to Chile's Anita Lizana.

Alice took no pleasure in JaJa's defeat. She was still trying to figure out what had gone wrong with her game. Teach said, "It's not your game. It's *you*. It's something in your head. You're number one in the country, yet you're playing as if you think you're a loser. What's wrong with you, Alice?"

Alice couldn't answer. Something had shifted inside her. She felt that of the two *me's*, the "weak one" from the sanatorium had taken over. Meanwhile, the "strong one" had slipped away somewhere. By the time she and Teach returned to California, Alice had thoughts of quitting tennis.

That idea grew in her when, shortly after her return, Dan phoned to say that their mother had died. Everyone in the family had been present—except Alice. Tennis had kept her from her mother's side. "Why did I let it happen?" Alice asked herself.

Teach was gentle with her, even when Alice told her that she wanted to bow out of the game. "The Pacific Southwest Tennis Championships is coming up," Teach said. "I know you can win—"

Alice began, "I know I can't—"

Teach interrupted, "All right. But give it a try. Please? And then we'll see. Okay?"

Alice sighed and nodded her head. "Okay."

When the tournament came, her skills carried her easily through the first rounds. Yet she felt empty, joyless. Her mood darkened further, the morning of the final match. Her opponent was Gracyn Wheeler, who had beaten her not long before. Alice began to feel she was going to lose to Gracyn.

Held at the Los Angeles Tennis Club, the Pacific Southwest Tennis Championships attracted socialites and movie personalities among other tennis fans. Alice knew that Carole Lombard was coming for the finals, escorted by Clark Gable. Alice had met that movie idol through Carole and had grown to know and like him. As she finished dressing, she thought it would cheer her to say hello to them both. There was time to stop at their box before the match.

As she threaded her way through the crowd, people called out friendly greetings. With nods and smiles, she passed them, until she stood behind the box reserved for Carole and Clark, her hand at its curtain. She heard Clark say, "You mustn't be upset if Alice loses, Carole, honey. We all love her, but let's face it. These days, she just hasn't got what it takes."

Carole murmured a protest, but Alice didn't wait to hear it. Red in the face, she fled back the way she'd come.

For some people in Alice's low spirits, Clark Gable's words would have been the final blow. For Alice, they had the opposite effect. Anger raced through her veins like a tonic. Trembling with rage, she thought, "So I don't have what it takes, huh? What in the world would *Clark* know about it?" He'd been a poor boy, then a lumberjack, then an actor. How many tennis games had he even *seen?* "I'll show that smug fool!" Alice thought.

She longed to punch the actor in his million-dollar face. If not for Carole, she might have done it. Instead, her fight went into her game. Gracyn Wheeler was a stylish player, but she didn't have a chance to show it. Alice mopped up the court with a dazed Gracyn at lightning speed. The score was 6–0, 6–0.

■ ■ ■

Eyes shining, Teach waited for Alice in the dressing room. "Well, Miss Sourpuss!" she exclaimed. "Still want to quit?" In answer, Alice simply threw her arms around Teach.

"The only thing I *really* want to do," she said a moment later, "is to sock that bum Gable in the jaw!"

Teach said, "Oh? As thanks for a box of lovely red roses?"

The card on the roses said, "To the champ of champs!"

Had the box been there before the match? Alice wondered. Maybe she'd been too depressed to notice. Maybe, in what she'd overheard, Clark had only been teasing Carole.

Alice would never know for sure—and she didn't care. She felt that she owed Clark Gable her second comeback. For on that day, all the spirit and power she thought she'd lost came back into her game. Afterward, she would lose only one singles match ever again in her entire amateur career.

CHAPTER 6

A Thread Comes Loose

At the New York dock, horns blasted and whistles shrieked. Reporters yelled last-minute questions. A crowd of friends and fans pressed forward for a better look at Alice and her coach. The two tall, well-dressed women—the blond head higher than the silver one—smiled into the flashing cameras.

Teach's smile was especially bright. She could never get enough of the fame and glory. She had her champ back, better than ever—and they were off to Wimbledon again!

Yes, off again, on a luxury liner. Again they were the center of a crowd of fashionable people—some of them empty-headed, some interesting, but all with one thing in common. All were rich themselves or had contacts among the rich.

As for Alice, it wasn't riches that had brought her into such company, but fame. Her fortunes hadn't changed since her second comeback. The only thing that had changed was that while she remained poor, she now lived almost entirely in the world of the rich.

There was another thing that hadn't changed. Although in this summer of 1938 Alice was nearly twenty-five, Teach still firmly controlled her life, almost as if she were a child. In many ways, Alice was a strong-willed person, even a stubborn one. Seeing her obedient behavior with Teach, a close friend might have wondered when Alice would break free of Teach's iron rule. But Alice had no close friends except Carole—and Brownie, whom she seldom saw. And Carole, although she often teased Alice about Teach's over-control, never spoke about it in a serious way.

Whatever the case, this year, as on the 1937 voyage, Alice kept away from shipboard romances. She went to sleep dutifully at ten, rose early to exercise, and kept to her diet. She looked as fit as Teach desired to reporters who met them in England.

Alice's highest hope was not for romance, anyway. It was that *this* year she would carry off the world championship at Wimbledon. By the time she reached the place, with its fresh-smelling greenery, its crowds of women in floppy straw hats and men in flannel trousers, she was in a state of high excitement.

The famous "two Helens" were in this year's contest—Helen Jacobs and Helen Wills Moody. Alice joked with Teach about the horrifying possibility that she might need to face them *both*. A joke of that kind showed how confident Alice felt: she was ready to knock over the two great Helens, if she had to.

Alice swept through the quarterfinal, defeating the French champion Simone Mathieu. This meant that in the semifinal she did, indeed, face a Helen. It was her friend Helen Jacobs, from whom Alice had unexpectedly taken the U.S. championship in 1936.

At Wimbledon in 1938, however, things turned out differently. Helen began to outplay Alice in the very first set. By the second set, Alice was unnerved. When her famous smash failed her, she became angry. Savagely, she kicked a ball into the stands.

A nervous cackle rose from the crowd. Alice's open display of temper was unusual at polite Wimbledon. Thrown off her concentration, Alice began playing for laughs. It was easy work for Helen to polish her off in the second set, 6–4, 6–4.

Alice was worse than heartsick—she was ashamed. She'd

behaved like a fool, like a child. Never again! she vowed. Surprisingly, however, Teach said nothing about her clowning. She said merely, "It's no disgrace to lose to Helen Jacobs."

So it was the "two Helens" who fought the singles final. Jacobs, who had injured her leg badly, lost to the older Helen Wills Moody. (Not long after that, the older Helen retired, ending her many years as queen of international tennis.)

Alice won the women's doubles title with Sarah Palfrey. Then she and Don Budge took the mixed doubles title for the second year in a row, scoring 6–1, 6–4.

A famous name in tennis history, Don Budge was a warm admirer of Alice. They were to team up for many exhibition matches in the near future. In an interview years later, Don explained the unique benefits of pairing with Alice:

> Alice was so special because she played like a man. At that time there was no woman who played anything near like a man. They played a ladies' game—darn good, but it didn't have the pressure or the pace that Alice could put on the balls. In many mixed doubles matches a lob'll go up, and the man'll say, "mine," and he'll take a ball that normally would be the lady's. But he has more power and strength, so he can put the ball away, whereas a lady might not. But Alice could handle her own.

Alice left Wimbledon 1938 with two of three championships. She was pleased now. Deeply as she longed for that singles title, she "felt in her bones" that in 1939, she'd win it.

Her bones gave her no sign of a more important fact about 1939. It was American ambassador Joseph Kennedy who did that. Amid the gaiety of the Wimbledon Ball, he said: "My girl, if you're going to win this thing, you'd better do it soon. There's going to be a war that will make all of us forget about tennis."

. . .

Teach thought it was time now for a bit of relaxation. Teach's socialite friend Rosalind Bloomingdale Cowen had been with Teach and Alice at Wimbledon. Roz suggested they go for a week to Le Touquet, France, a gambling resort across the English Channel. Roz rented rooms for them, herself, and her sons at the best hotel. It had a big casino, where she and Teach could gamble away the hours. For Roz, whose first husband owned the Bloomingdale's department store chain, money was no problem.

Roz's oldest son, Alfred, was about Alice's age. Neither he nor Alice cared for gambling. Alfred wanted to chase girls, but not the kind that Roz would approve of. Alice wanted to be rid of Teach's gaze, free to wander the colorful seaport town at will. Like two children, she and Alfred made a pact: if any questions were asked, they'd tell the "adults" they'd been with each other.

The day after the group's arrival, Alfred found a girl. He made a date with her for that evening. He and Alice left the hotel together after dining with Teach and Roz. They parted a few blocks away. Alice went to a movie—she was able to follow its well-worn plot, even though she didn't know French. She then returned to the hotel, where she seated herself in the lobby.

It was a pleasure just to bask in the mellow light of the hanging crystal lamps, to gaze at the ornate furniture and the Oriental rugs. She also liked to watch the elegant people as they moved in and out of the casino, the restaurants and bars. "You mustn't *stare*," her mother probably would have said.

Since Alice's face was known, people sometimes stared at

her. As she sat in her chair, she sensed someone watching her. Looking up, her blue eyes met a pair of darker blue.

"It is Miss Marble, yes?" The eyes and the voice belonged to a smiling young man in a well-cut tuxedo. "But of course it is you!" he exclaimed. "I have just seen you play, at Wimbledon. Oh, I admire your tennis so much, Miss Marble."

Alice said, "Why, thank you." She felt suddenly glad that the filmy dress she was wearing was one of her favorites. The man's blond looks were striking, even to Alice, who had spent her time among many handsome screen stars. To her confusion, she felt herself blushing. She looked down at the carpet.

"Allow me to introduce myself! I am Kurt Bergner."*

He bowed, took the hand she held out, and kissed it. Now she nearly laughed. The scene was too much like the corny movie she had just watched. But she didn't care—and she did laugh. "I've played better tennis than I did in the singles semifinal."

"You will win it next year," Kurt said. "Everyone knows." Glancing about, he said, "Are you meeting someone? If not, would you come and talk with me over a drink?"

Alice glanced around the lobby, too. What if Teach were to see her? Then she thought: "So *what?* I'm a grown woman!" She rose. "I'll be glad to—unless you mind my drinking iced tea."

In the bar, Alice learned that Kurt was from Geneva, Switzerland. His father, who was German, owned a bank there. Kurt worked for the bank and traveled frequently on business. It was clear that he also traveled for pleasure. He spoke of ski trips in Austria and of swimming and boating

---

*Not his actual name. In her autobiography, Alice disguised the man's name and described him as dark-haired rather than blond.

on the coasts of France, Italy, and Greece. He followed sports as a spectator, too. That, and some business in London, was what had brought him to Wimbledon.

"And Le Touquet? Are you a gambler?" Alice asked.

Kurt shrugged. "A little. It's also a lovely spot, nice beaches. I'll show you one nearby, if you like. I think you'd prefer a beach walk to the casino. Yes?"

In the dim light, Alice tried to read her watch. Kurt saw, and laughed. "Nobody ever goes to sleep here. Come."

Alice could easily have read the lobby clock as they passed through to the outer doors. She did not trouble to do so. She was beyond worrying about Teach. It was as if she'd been sipping gin instead of iced tea. She felt drunk with excitement.

Dangling her high-heeled slippers in her hand, she strolled beside Kurt in the sand. "How bright the stars are!" she said. Kurt slipped an arm around her waist. "Shall we stop and look at them?" She nodded.

He flung his tuxedo jacket onto the sand. "Like Walter Raleigh," he said. "For a queen much lovelier than Elizabeth."

Alice knew what was going to happen. She wanted it to happen. Alice had been introduced to sex in a particularly horrible way. But that was years ago. It had nothing to do with the overwhelming attraction she felt for Kurt. What she felt for Kurt belonged to her. She was ready for it and it was right.

Before they parted, they made a date for the following day, at noon. It was, of course, already the "following day," as the clock in the lobby informed her.

Now all her fears rushed back. She could only hope that Roz and Teach were still in the casino. She put the key in the lock of the suite she and Teach shared and gently pushed the door.

Still dressed in her evening clothes, Teach was seated in a

chair. Her eyes took in Alice's messy hair and makeup. In a voice of ice, she said: "I trust you've had a nice evening?"

It took only a few minutes for Alice to fall to pieces. Her voice trembled as she began: "I have a right to my own life—"

"Oh, do you, now?" Teach rose and grabbed Alice by the arm. Her nails dug into it. "And who the hell gave you the life you have? Who paid the bills when you were sick as a dog?"

Alice began to cry. "My God, Teach—I get—get lonely!"

Teach shook her. "Answer me! Who stuck by you when everybody thought you were finished? Who put up with you? Even last year, when you couldn't win a tournament! Who? Who? *Who*?"

Alice blurted out, "You!" She sobbed into her hands.

"Yet you'll fall into the arms of any man who asks?" Teach blasted at her. "I've brought you all this way—and now you're at the top of your game! But men and tennis don't mix! If you don't believe me—bye-bye. I won't waste time on a fool!"

"I'm sorry," Alice whispered.

"Hardly enough! Do you promise it's the last time?"

"I promise," Alice said. She looked Teach in the eye as she said it. Then she entered her own room and went to bed.

But she didn't intend to keep her promise—not even before the roses from Kurt arrived for her at breakfast. She and Alfred had made their plans in the hallway before joining Roz and Teach at their hotel table. Having lied to Teach a few hours before, Alice was able to pretend now that the card on the roses said only, "From a devoted fan." She left it to Alfred to tell "the adults" that they'd be gone all day on a picnic together.

As it happened, she did go on a picnic—with Kurt. It was the first of a series of outings that lasted most of the week. Alice and Alfred parted from the "adults" at breakfast, giving one story or another about their plans for the day and evening. Meanwhile, Kurt moved into a room on the floor above Alice's. Returning from a day's outing to countryside woods, rivers, or castles, he and Alice re-entered the hotel separately. They then met in Kurt's room, where they spent their afternoons together. Alice didn't want any of it to end, ever. She floated rosily on a dream that maybe it never would. . . .

One afternoon, Alfred slipped a hasty note under Kurt's door: "Alice—photo of you and Kurt on society page. Teach might see." The photo had been snapped at an inn where Alice and Kurt had stopped for lunch the day before.

Teach had, indeed, seen. She had finished dressing for dinner when Alice entered their suite. Picking up her beaded evening bag, she said shortly: "Tell Bergner it's over."

"Teach . . . what can I . . . I can't, I—"

"You can and you will." Teach's voice was toneless. "End it." She opened the door. "Or get yourself another coach."

She closed the door without slamming it. Alice sat and stared at it, seeing nothing. Her thoughts were a jumble. She didn't cry. She sat for an hour, thinking, until her mind cleared. Then she dragged herself to her feet and went upstairs to Kurt's room.

Kurt opened the door to her knock. His blond hair was wet from the comb, and he smelled of shaving lotion. He took her in his arms and kissed the top of her head. "Pretty bad, was it?" he said.

His voice was a little amused. He'd never understood why their meetings had to be kept a secret from Alice's coach. Alice had tried to explain what she owed Teach, but had given it up. Kurt had never had to go without clothes he needed, never feared snobbery and scorn, never worried about doctors' bills—never been poor, in short. He'd gone along with Alice's secrecy, but he couldn't help seeing it as a kind of joke. Now he said:

"She'll calm down, dearest. Surely she must know that she can't keep a wonderful creature like you—a goddess!—locked up forever! She'll come to her senses, and then, when I get to New York, I can talk to her, I'll tell her how much I love you—"

"It won't do any good." Alice's voice was as toneless as Teach's had been. "There's no point in following me to New York. I can't see you. It would mean giving up Teach—and tennis."

Kurt grew silent. Then he said, "You'd rather give me up."

"No, no! Don't say that! I love *you*! Only—she saved my life, she made me a champion." Alice had begun to cry. "I can't just—tear it all up. I can't do that to her!"

Kurt held Alice tightly. He bent and kissed her lips. Then he looked at her for a long moment. "Goodbye, my darling Alice," he said.

She turned away, barged out the door, and fled along the hall before she could change her mind.

The next day, Kurt was gone. Once Teach was sure of that, she had the decency to leave Alice to herself. Alice found beaches where she could weep in privacy. By the time she and Teach were homeward bound, she had emptied herself of tears. As their ship crossed the Atlantic toward New York, she began talking with Teach about the upcoming U.S. championship tournament. They spoke normally, as if nothing had changed.

But a change had taken place. For the first time, she had deceived Teach. She had defied her. A thread had come loose in the weave that bound her and Teach together. It would never be as strong again.

CHAPTER 7

The View from the Top

Alice spent the summer as she had expected, hard at work on her tennis. She was preparing for the U.S. championships. Sometimes her heart skipped a beat when she glimpsed a tall, fair-haired figure at a distance. She knew quite well that Kurt would not come to her in the United States unless she asked him to. At the same time, she couldn't accept the thought that she would never see him again. He waited always at the back of her mind, showing up in her dreams, or seeming to walk toward her down a street.

The 1938 championships at Forest Hills proved a real test for Alice. She and Sarah Palfrey won the women's doubles title, but they had to fight hard for it. Then Alice nearly lost the singles semifinal to Sarah. Sarah's playing was so brilliant that day that Alice scarcely believed her own narrow final win: 5–7, 7–5, 7–5.

After that, it seemed almost easy to regain her national singles crown. In twenty minutes, she beat Australian champion Nancy Wynne 6–0, 6–3. With her celebrated partner Don Budge, she also won the mixed doubles. She had earned a triple crown!

This sweeping victory reaped a hurricane of public attention. By now, she and Teach were used to handling it. They stayed on in New York for the familiar interviews, newsreels, photo sessions, radio shows, and speaking dates. There was something entirely new this time, however: a talent agency asked Alice to try out for a singing job.

Alice had sung often at private parties. Urged by Carole Lombard, and at Carole's expense, she'd taken voice lessons. But she had long ago given up her youthful dreams of a singing career. The person who had suggested her for this job was Emil Coleman, a band leader. He'd listened to Alice's singing at a party one night and had liked her voice.

Teach objected to the idea. But Alice couldn't help being thrilled. The job was at the Waldorf-Astoria Hotel, a famed and glamorous setting. Ignoring Teach's frown, she went to the tryout. She was offered the job—and accepted it. It was the first paid work she'd had—except for odd jobs as a child—that she didn't owe to Teach. And the salary was very large.

The next two months were like a movie—with a star who didn't feel much like Alice Marble. This star was given a suite at the Waldorf even before her opening night. True, she had to spend a lot of her pay on evening gowns for appearances. She also paid a singing coach, and a song arranger for each number.

It all seemed worthwhile when she opened at the Waldorf. Five hundred people jammed the opening. She later remarked, in her autobiography, that a fair number of them were her friends. Still, to her pleasure, their enthusiasm was echoed by good reviews in the New York newspapers the following day.

A lot of her tennis fans didn't share the enthusiasm for Alice's work in a nightclub. It didn't seem the right setting for a sports heroine like Alice, the "clean-cut American girl." Some fans didn't approve of "nightlife"—late hours, smoking, and drinking—at least, not for their athletes. It wasn't healthy.

After a while, Alice began to agree. It was hard to practice tennis every day when she'd been up half the night. And being a professional singer wasn't easy. As an athlete, Alice tried to hide her emotions from the crowd and her opponents. It wasn't good to let them see if you felt discouraged or too cocky. But you had to learn to *show* feelings to put over a song.

Most important, she needed to train in earnest if she aimed to win the Wimbledon singles crown in 1939. Realizing that she couldn't manage both careers at once, she gave up singing.

■ ■ ■

In 1939, Alice Marble was at the peak of her game. She knew it, and few doubted it when she arrived in England. "Alice Marvel," the newspapers there had begun to call her. People said that a feeling like an electric shock ran through the stands as soon as Alice stepped onto a court.

In the Wimbledon singles semifinal, Alice faced Hilda Sperling, of Denmark. A tall, thin woman with enormously long arms and legs, Hilda looked something like a spider. The greatest players feared her swift and deadly accuracy. Yet in twenty minutes, Alice had defeated her 6–0, 6–0.

Nobody had ever beaten Hilda so quickly and so completely. She was broken-hearted. Alice found her crying in their dressing room. She put her arms around Hilda. She cried, too.

Seeing them, nobody could have guessed which of them had lost. Teach used to tell people that Alice was "not a killer."

Alice went on to play the semifinals of the mixed doubles with Bobby Riggs as her partner. Teach was Bobby's coach, too. They won, but reaching for a ball, Alice tore a stomach muscle. She was in terrible pain when she woke the next morning.

It was the day of her singles final, as well as the women's

doubles. Despite the pain, it was out of the question not to play. Maybe she wasn't a "killer," but she had a giant will to win. With her torso taped by a doctor, she went out to face her opponent—and friend—Britain's Kay Stammers.

Some people had stood all night in the rain to get a seat for this final. Their reward was near-flawless tennis. Kay was a daring and highly skilled player. Gritting her teeth and ignoring the pain, Alice nevertheless anticipated Kay's every move. She wrung from herself each needed counter-move. It was all over quickly. Alice won 6–2, 6–0.

Very little sound came from the stands. The spectators were stunned. At the net, Alice was somewhat stunned, herself. Kay was hugging her. Then the red carpet was rolled from the royal box. Alice stepped forward on the American ambassador's arm to meet the Dowager Queen Mary.

"It was the greatest moment of my life," Alice later wrote. She took from the smiling Queen's hands the shining gold trophy. She wished her mother were alive so that she could take the trophy home to her. She thought of her brother Dan, who had started her on the road that had led to this moment. He would be so proud when he learned the news. And Teach! Engulfed by reporters, Teach was ecstatic.

That same day, with Sarah Palfrey, Alice won the women's doubles. She and Bobby Riggs won the mixed doubles in straight sets. For both of them, it was a clean sweep: singles, doubles, and mixed doubles. Alice was the first woman in the century to win all three Wimbledon crowns in the same year. No one but Bobby had ever won all three events on the first try.

The tennis world recognized the huge triumph for Teach, who had coached them both. She said, "It's the most rewarding day of my life." Bobby—known for his arrogance long before his 1973 defeat by Billie Jean King—told Alice why *he* felt pleased. The odds against his winning all three events were overwhelming, he said. He'd bet his every dime on himself—and made a pile.

It was unsporting, and it was his way of showing off. Alice was used to it. She'd practiced with him many times since Teach became his coach. He was a no-good rascal in her opinion. But as they led off the first dance as queen and king of the Wimbledon Ball, she was so happy, she could only laugh.

Dancing in a red gown she'd bought for her Waldorf job and wearing high heels, Alice was taller than Bobby. Together, they paused for a memorable photograph. Memorable, because in less than eight weeks, World War II would begin. Although few of those present were aware of it, international tennis was coming to a halt. The group in the ballroom was a gathering of people with a common interest, coming together from many nations. It would not happen again for a long time.

Alice Marble's successful fight for the world tennis championship had been her final chance to win it. A few short weeks after that, she had to defend her U.S. title. On a day of strong winds, she faced Helen Jacobs for the singles final at Forest Hills. Both were marvelous players, but neither knew where the wind would carry their shots. For an hour and a half, they battled the weather and each other. When Alice ended as the winner, she thought it might have been pure chance.

Yet once again she made a triple sweep of the championships. With Australian Harry Hopman, she won the mixed doubles. She and Sarah Palfrey teamed to win the women's doubles. Kay Stammers was one of their opponents. Tears in her eyes, Alice hugged Kay. If Britain went to war, when would they meet again?

On September 1, 1939, Hitler's troops marched into Poland. France and Great Britain immediately declared war on

Germany. The U.S. did not officially enter the war until Japanese planes bombed Pearl Harbor, toward the end of 1941. Before that, however, the first peacetime military draft in U.S. history was put into effect. The country was gearing up for another world war. For seven years, few foreign tennis players came to its shores.

But the U.S. national championships continued. Recently named Woman Athlete of the Year by sportswriters, Alice competed again in 1940. She held to her triple sweep for the third time, remaining the champion of all events. In the singles final, she again defeated Helen Jacobs—although, as usual, it wasn't easy.

They exchanged personal news after the match. Helen was hoping to enter one of the newly created women's military units. Teach wanted Alice to go into professional tennis. But Alice felt it was almost childish to be playing tennis in these times. She thought perhaps she should enter the military herself.

Teach lost her temper when Alice mentioned it. After her Wimbledon triumph, Alice had turned down fabulous offers from major movie studios. If Alice wanted to do something besides tennis, why not something that could make them rich?

Alice didn't argue with Teach, but went ahead and applied for the Women's Army Corps. To her amazement, she was turned down as "unfit." Looking into her health records, the recruiting office discovered that she'd had tuberculosis. It seemed not to matter that her health was perfect now, or that she was a world champion athlete. "Those are our regulations," she was told. She got the same news from every armed forces branch.

She began to feel she wasn't fit to do anything except hit a tennis ball. She was ignorant in everything but sports. Dan had been right, she thought, in wanting her to get an education. Not knowing where to start, she took a Spanish course at night.

Teach returned to the subject of professional tennis. With international sports events stopped by the war, amateur tennis had lost its glitter. But amateur stars were in demand for paid tours, especially male stars. Teach had been getting offers for Alice to join the men pros since her 1937 Wimbledon win with Don.

Alice told Teach she'd think about it. Instead, she thought about joining the Red Cross. Brownie planned to do that soon.

One day Alice answered the phone in the New York apartment she and Teach shared. A voice said: "Miss Marble? This is the White House calling. Please hold." Then over the line came the familiar voice of President Franklin D. Roosevelt.

Alice's hand on the receiver shook a little as she listened. She nodded her head. "Yes, Mr. President. Certainly, sir . . . Yes, of course, sir . . . Thank you, Mr. President."

She sank into a chair. "Teach!" she cried weakly. Teach appeared in the doorway. "Oh, Teach—it was President Roosevelt! He asked me to co-chair a physical fitness program for the Office of Civilian Defense! Teach! Would you be my assistant?"

"It's an honor," Teach said. "*You* can't say no. But I can. Those honor positions pay a dollar a year. Did you know?"

But Brownie didn't hesitate when Alice phoned. Letting another teacher take over her college classes, she joined Alice.

There was a flurry of publicity: wire service stories, photos of Alice and Brownie in their new uniforms. If she and Brownie had merely wanted publicity for themselves, that might have been enough. But their chief aim was to interest civilians in the values of keeping physically fit. Hitting the road from their Washington, D.C., office, they met group after group. Many were interested in seeing Alice Marble; few were interested in attending physical fitness classes. Alice and Brownie gave it their best try—before they gave up.

Brownie returned to her plan to work for the Red Cross. With a sad feeling, Alice hung her uniform in a closet. She told Teach she was ready to sign for a pro tour. Teach beamed.

The tour opened January 6, 1941, to a packed crowd in New York's Madison Square Garden. Other team members were Mary Hardwick Hare, of Great Britain, and Don Budge. All-time tennis great Bill Tilden, now close to fifty, made the fourth. The tour went on to seventy more cities and another seventy-five matches, booked almost on top of each other. It was exhausting—but at its end, Alice and Teach were one hundred thousand dollars richer.

That was a very large sum for 1941. It would have been a lot smaller, had Alice not acted without Teach's advice. Teach had signed a twenty-five thousand dollar contract for Alice. But Alice soon discovered that other team members were being paid a great deal more. On the tour's third stop, she demanded equal pay to Don Budge's—seventy-five thousand and a cut of profits.

"Otherwise," said Alice, "I'm not playing." The head of the tour's sponsoring company said, "We'll sue you."

"Go ahead," Alice replied. Although it was long before the existence of laws backing equal pay for women, Alice wasn't worried. With seventy-three bookings to go, and no player distinguished enough to replace her, she knew she'd get her way.

She got her way, and for a while after the tour ended, she was very pleased with herself. For the first time, she had managed the business end of her career without Teach's help. She was happy, too, that she could repay Teach with some real money. In fact, before the tour, she'd also made a nice sum from a short-term singing act at a New York theater.

But she felt restless and guilty at news of what was going on in the world. In Germany and the countries it had conquered, the Nazis' persecution of Jews became more brutal and open. Many Americans believed the answer to Nazi violence was to support the war against Germany. Alice felt the same.

So she joined Don, Mary, and Bill on another tennis tour. This time, the purpose wasn't to make money. It was to entertain troops at military bases. After the United States was actually at war with both Germany and Japan, the tour did make money. But the money wasn't for the players—the millions they raised from the general public went to U.S. War Bonds.

Carole Lombard was also making tours of military bases. She and Alice continued to be close. It was to Carole alone, during a stay in Los Angeles, that Alice had spoken about Kurt. The two friends kept in touch through letters and phone calls.

Alice was therefore filled with grief when Carole was killed in an airplane crash. Carole's death meant that Alice lost one of the only two people she confided in. Brownie was the other. Brownie at least was with Alice more often now; for between her Red Cross missions, she stayed with Alice and Teach in New York.

Knowing that many were losing their lives and loved ones to war, Alice buried her personal grief. She began to tour military hospitals, singing, playing cards, and talking with the wounded. She also regularly visited and sang at New York's Stage Door Canteen, a famed social club for men and women in uniform.

It was there, on a winter night, ending a song, that she met the man she was to marry.

CHAPTER 8

More Peaks, Deeper Valleys

U.S. Army Captain Joseph Crowley wouldn't stand out in a crowd. He wasn't strikingly blond, like Kurt, or tall, dark, and handsome like the male movie idols of the day. He'd grown up on a Kansas farm, but he didn't have the rugged, sunburned look of a farmer. He was brown-haired and well built, and he had a sweet smile. And that was it. But out of all the uniformed men in the room, Alice recalled, "He was the only one I saw."

She saw him the minute he walked into the room—and directed her song to him, drawing him toward her. Standing at the piano, he requested a song: "Stardust." That wasn't unusual; it was a very popular tune. Then he asked if she would play ping-pong with him, and *that* wasn't unusual, either. Most of the visitors to the canteen challenged her to ping-pong: it was the closest they could get to a game of tennis with the great Alice Marble.

One thing was unusual, however. When Captain Crowley asked Alice to dinner, she said yes. She'd always gracefully refused dates at the canteen. She didn't want to refuse this one.

The next evening they sat across the table from each other. Alice only pretended to eat. The sight of him, the sound of his voice made her heart leap and her stomach flip-flop.

It didn't take long for Joe to tell her the facts of his life. He was twenty-five, three years younger than Alice. He had an engineering degree, was an air force pilot, and worked in army intelligence. The work was secret; he couldn't talk much about it. He never knew where he'd be going next. "I'm leaving tomorrow," he said. "Would you see me again when I come back?"

He didn't say, "*If* I come back." Alice supplied it herself. When she wasn't playing exhibition matches or doing her stints at hospitals and the canteen, she was listening for the phone. She said not a word about any of that to Teach. It was Brownie she told, during one of Brownie's visits to New York.

Brownie wasn't in town when, weeks later, Joe's phone call finally came. As it happened, Teach was also away. She couldn't see Alice's shining face when Alice at last heard Joe's voice.

Slipping into a new dress, brushing her hair joyfully, Alice decided it wouldn't have mattered to her if Teach *had* seen. Not now. She was so astonished by this thought that, hairbrush in hand, she sat down suddenly on the bed. It didn't matter!

She saw that for months, even years, she'd more and more been doing as she pleased. Maybe it had begun when she'd won the triple world championship? Anyway, now it seemed perfectly crazy that Teach believed that she had a right to run Alice's private life. Her professional life—that was different: Teach had created Alice's career. But she hadn't created Alice.

Tears came to Alice's eyes. Poor Teach! She wanted to *own* Alice—and Alice had almost let her. After all, she loved Teach. She'd be grateful to her forever. But . . . love or not, grateful or not—she was taking her life back!

■ ■ ■

In the same year they met, 1942, Alice Marble and Joseph Crowley were married. Alice kept her marriage a secret from the public for a long time. But she told Brownie about the wedding plans immediately, in a long-distance phone call. Brownie—who had helped Alice through anxious times between Joe's visits and letters—greeted the news with, "Hip, hip, hooray!" Then she asked, "Teach having fits?"

Brownie knew that Teach had *already* been having fits. Teach had stormed and screamed when she'd learned that Alice was seeing Joe Crowley regularly and guessed that their relationship was serious. In her rage, she had even kept Joe's messages from Alice sometimes. In spite of all that, Alice held firm against her.

Alice didn't tell Teach about her marriage. She didn't mention it to her friends generally, and not to the press. However, there were rumors about the marriage, and Teach must have heard them. She didn't admit it to Alice. They went on as before. Their tours continued, they stayed on at the same apartment in New York. When Joe came home, Alice simply disappeared for as long as he was free, the two of them living in hotel rooms.

Unlike most couples affected by military orders, there was no single dramatic moment for them when Joe was "sent overseas." He regularly went overseas. Each parting brought new sadness and the same question: "Will we ever see each other again?"

Between goodbyes, they behaved like any newly-weds. Each event was new and thrilling: waking up for breakfast together; holding hands as they walked and window-shopped; dancing close together at "our place," then slipping away to their hotel.

Joe's home leaves sometimes came when Alice was on a tour. He went along wherever she happened to be playing. He delighted in watching her matches. An all-around athlete, he sometimes served as Alice's practice partner. After seeing him often, for well over a year, Teach seemed to get used to his presence. At any rate, she greeted him in a normal tone instead of staring straight through him.

Alice and Joe enjoyed building dreams of a settled post-war life. "Mrs. Crowley," Joe said, trying out the sound, "Where would you like to live?" And, "How many children shall we have, Mrs. Crowley?" Alice said, "Well. A news columnist once said I should have twelve." Joe whistled. "It's a good thing you're rich!"

They didn't really expect it to happen. On the other hand, never knowing what the next day might bring, they were driven by an unspoken wish to cram their entire lives into *right now.* As a result, they weren't always careful about using birth control.

In New York between tour dates, Alice began to feel sick to her stomach every morning. A visit to the doctor confirmed that she was pregnant. She was as flushed with triumph as if she'd carried off another triple crown. Home on a day's leave, Joe was amazed, thrilled, full of plans and excitement. Even Teach—not much pleased about Alice's pregnancy—was amused as Joe, cross-legged on the living room floor of the New York apartment, paged the dictionary, asking opinions of boys' names and girls' names. The shadows lengthened, the brief hours fled. Jamming on his cap, crushing Alice in his arms, elated, laughing, Joe was gone.

Alice kept to her tours and practice. She felt fine. In her fifth month of pregnancy, she went to a party on Long Island, near New York City. Driving home, she was startled to see the lights of an oncoming car—on her side of the road. She felt the cruel impact of the steering wheel as her car went into a ditch.

Three days later she was taken home from a hospital by Teach and Brownie. She was not badly injured—but she had miscarried.

Joe was in the habit of phoning from overseas as often as he could. Alice said to Teach and Brownie, "If you answer the phone, please don't tell Joe. I don't want him to find out yet."

He never found out. On Christmas Eve, 1944, Alice received a telegram from the War Department. Joe had died in action. His plane had been shot down over Germany.

She was at first unbelieving. Never to see him again? Never, really, even getting to know him, all the dear things about him. If only, she thought, the baby had lived! She would then have something of Joe. Now she had nothing—nothing at all.

Ignoring Teach, and even Brownie, Alice crawled into bed and stayed there. As in Paris, when she'd been told at age twenty-one that she would never play tennis again, she wanted to die. At that time, she had prayed to die.

She didn't need to pray, now. On her bedside table was a bottle of sleeping pills. There were a lot, for she seldom used them. She swung her legs over the bed and went into the bathroom for water. It seemed to take a long time to get them down. . . . Once again, she woke in a hospital bed.

■ ■ ■

As she had at age twenty-one, after her breakdown in Paris, Alice Marble disappeared from public view. Not only did she not continue her tennis tours, she didn't even leave the apartment. Instead of getting plump, this time, she was painfully thin. Unable to force down a meal or sleep through a night, unable to focus on a book or a newspaper, she wandered from room to room.

Every once in a while a bit of information on the radio broke through to her: the war against Japan wasn't going well for the United States and its allies; the Germans, on the other hand, now seemed to be getting the worst of it. Alice's eyes filled with tears. *Her* war was over. She hoped the suffering would end soon for others.

Brownie and Teach tried to tempt her out of the apartment. They never left her alone there. Alice told them, "You don't have to watch me. I won't try it again. I've given you trouble enough."

It was Carole Lombard who revived Alice's will to live— so Alice believed. Carole, who was gone, led Alice back to herself—for the second time, at second hand. One day a box of red roses came from Clark Gable. He'd enlisted in the air force after Carole's death. His card said: "If I can do it, so can you."

They were Carole's words, sent to Alice years before in the sanatorium. Wanting to believe it, Alice felt sure that Carole was trying to speak to her through Clark. She looked up from the roses. "Brownie," she said, "I'm taking you to lunch." She phoned a club where Teach was giving tennis clinics. Naming a costly restaurant, she said to Teach: "Noon. And it's on me."

Alice had turned a corner that day. She was aware that she was still mostly going through the motions of living. Yet she also knew, from her earlier depression, that if she kept at it, she would one day notice that they were no longer the mere motions of living, but living itself. It was very much like sticking to the tennis strokes Beese had taught her. They had seemed so foreign, so strange, even *wrong*. Yet as she doggedly practiced them, they began to feel familiar—until at last she was using them naturally, as if they'd been hers all along.

There was one thing, however, that hadn't happened before. It was a thing that bothered her badly. She'd begun to feel that she was being *followed*. "Am I going crazy?" she thought.

It was therefore almost a relief when the man she believed had been following her sat down beside her on a bench in Central Park. "Miss Marble," he said, "I'm Captain Smith."*

---

*Not the captain's real name.

"Yes?" Alice's voice was cautious. "Captain of what?" she asked herself. The man wasn't in uniform.

She later understood why he was in street clothes. The meeting was the first of many secret meetings she would have with members of a U.S. Army Intelligence team. Her life now became like a fictional spy thriller. Only this was a real-life one.

Five years earlier, when Alice had been appointed to the Office of Civilian Defense, her past had been carefully checked. The government had learned all there was to know about her—including her affair with Kurt. That affair had become important because, she was told, it might enable her to spy on him now.

Spy on *Kurt*? "What *for*?" Alice asked when she met Captain Smith's commanding officer, a colonel. He explained that it was because of Kurt's links with highly placed Nazis, through his bank in war-neutral Switzerland. These Nazis had been sending to Kurt's bank, for safe-keeping, art treasures and other valuables seized from Jews and other Nazi victims. If Germany lost the war, Kurt's Nazi clients planned to smuggle the wealth to countries where they might make a fresh start.

"But what's it to do with *me*?" Alice asked. "Am I supposed to ask for a tour of his bank and then sneak out the treasures?"

"It's unlikely many are kept in the bank," the colonel said. "No, what we want are Kurt Bergner's records. The lists of the valuables, the names of the Nazis who expect to get them after the war."

He went on, "We suspect Bergner wouldn't keep the records at the bank. More likely a private place, like his home." Turning pink, he added: "We think you can get invited to stay with him."

Each step that followed this conversation seemed to Alice

more and more unreal, like a B-movie. Her "cover" was to be some exhibition tennis matches set up for her in Switzerland. She was to tell no one her real purpose. The mission was dangerous; and past a point, she might be on her own. She'd be trained in body-contact self-defense and in the use of a gun. She had to learn other skills, too: use of a special spy camera and safe-cracking.

Alice thought: "They're telling me I could get killed." *That* was real. On the other hand . . . she detested everything she knew about Nazism. If there was anything she could do to stop its spread, wasn't it her duty to do it? Joe had been willing to die—was dead. "I'll do it," she said.

Everything happened as had been hoped. Kurt saw the news of her visit and contacted her. In a few days, she was staying with him at his family castle. He occupied it alone, except for servants. On a tour with him of his wine cellar, she spotted his private vault. What was more, she discovered where he kept its key. He even left her alone one night, reluctantly, to attend an important social event. She'd pretended she had a cold.

As in a dream, or a movie, when he'd left and the servants had gone to sleep, she slipped down to the cellar. She was armed with her camera, her gun, and the vault key. Getting into the vault easily, she found a neat ledger with row after row of German names and lists of stolen treasures—many surrounding her in the vault. She went to work on the ledger with her camera.

Before she had quite finished, she heard Kurt's eager voice. "Alice? Darling, I'm back!" His footsteps raced upstairs.

Alice fled from the cellar and out the front door. She leaped into Kurt's Mercedes. Its key was in the lock.

It was as she roared along a dark mountain road that the dream became a nightmare. She saw that she was being chased by another car. It caught up with her and roared alongside her. Terrified, she allowed her eyes to slide toward its driver.

The driver was Captain Smith. "Oh, thank God!" She pulled to the side of the road, clutched the camera, and tottered toward him.

Something was wrong with this movie. Captain Smith didn't seem welcoming. He said, "Give me the camera." Alice replied, "But—but I'm supposed to give the film to our Geneva contact!"

"Change of plans," said Smith. "Give it to me."

In that moment, Alice understood that Smith was a double agent. As he grappled with her for the camera, it fell to the ground. He put his foot on it, pulling his gun on her. She reached for her gun—but it wasn't with her. It was in the car.

She turned and ran. She felt the bullet entering her back. As she fell to the ground, she made out sounds—the squeal of brakes, another gun going off. Then everything went blank.

CHAPTER 9

A Long Way

After a pause, Alice's dream/movie went on. As she'd often done in the past, she woke in a hospital, this time on an army base. In true Hollywood style, the hero escaped death.

To be correct, the hero of a 1940s action movie would have had to be a man. Otherwise, everything was standard. The U.S. intelligence people had suspected that Smith was a double agent. As Smith followed Alice's car, he was himself followed by the colonel and other U.S. intelligence officers. They shot and killed him—although not soon enough to protect Alice. Still, she was alive.

The colonel didn't like telling Alice the *bad* news. It was that Captain Smith, before he was shot, had opened the camera. He'd exposed the film, erasing Alice's record of Nazi crimes.

Once more as in a spy thriller, the last twist was the best. Alice said that *she* had the information they wanted—in her brain. Her photographic memory held the records she'd taken from the ledger's pages. Now she "read" them aloud to U.S. secret agency stenographers to record, page by page.

Mission accomplished! All she needed to do now was recover from her wound. She was told she might travel in another month.

The colonel held Alice's hand warmly when he said goodbye. "You deserve a medal for courage. Unfortunately, all this must be kept secret. Maybe when the war is over . . ." He gave her hand a final squeeze. "For now, we'll see you get home safely."

She returned to New York the first week of May 1945. Only days afterward, the European war ended in victory for the United States and its allies. Three months later, after the United States rained atomic death and ruin on the cities of Hiroshima and Nagasaki, Japan also surrendered. That fall, with her war-time Red Cross service over, Brownie went home to Ohio. Alice was sorry to see her go. It had been a comfort to have Brownie around, even though Alice could not confide in her as she longed to do. The interlude with Kurt had left Alice deeply troubled. He had been so joyous, thinking he'd won her back. At some level, she felt she had betrayed him.

But what did it matter, she thought—a man like that! Then she drew back from the thought, asking herself: a man like *what*? From his own point of view, Kurt was simply doing "business as usual." No doubt his dealings with the Nazis were legal in Switzerland: the Swiss were not at war with Germany. A shrewd banker, Kurt had made money off the Nazis. Probably he'd asked no questions about their wealth. Yet he must have known that it came from the victims of Nazi mass murders and concentration camps. It cut Alice to the heart that Kurt had been able to ignore that. She felt confused and wretched that she'd loved him.

Yet Alice did not feel the least bit confused about why she had done what *she'd* done. If she were asked, she thought, she'd do it again—although she hoped she wouldn't be asked!

She felt highly rewarded a few months later. In November 1945, the trial of German war criminals began. The International Military Tribunal was held at Nuremberg, Germany, with evidence given against the accused. Alice's list played its part. Like her role later in *Pat and Mike*, a 1952 film with Spencer Tracey and Katherine Hepburn, it was a bit part. Unlike that movie role, her part in the Nuremberg trials was anonymous. But, for Alice, it was enough.

After Brownie's departure, Alice and Teach's relationship grew worse and worse. Brownie had acted as a buffer between them. Now Teach let her watchful jealousy come out in full force. She wanted Alice to account for each minute spent away from her. She drank heavily, threatened to kill herself, made scenes in front of their friends. Alice did what she could to calm her—but she refused to go back to being Teach's property.

In the end, Teach returned to California—but not before she had drawn all the money from the joint bank account she and Alice had. Alice could have stopped her, but didn't. Teach's theft helped Alice feel she'd squared much of her debt to Teach. In addition, Teach's fame as a coach had spread worldwide. With the reputation she'd gained because of Alice, Teach could take her pick of champion-class players. She could make a pile of money coaching and managing a new star.

Alice was glad to be free of Teach's frantic attempts to own her. That didn't stop her from trying to remain friends with Teach—as an equal. She wrote Teach, she tried to reach her by phone. But equality wasn't Teach's way. It was all or nothing.

With regret, Alice abandoned her efforts. She launched zestfully into a new life. She made new friends, women and men with a broad range of interests and talents. To fill her hunger to learn more of the world than could be gained on a tennis court, she attended classes at New York University. Urged by friends and fans, in 1946 she published an autobiography. In that book, as in many of her activities—teaching tennis clinics, coaching, lecturing—she did her best to help younger players.

Among these younger players was the first (and, for years, the only) black world tennis champion, the great Althea Gibson. In Althea Gibson's autobiography, she makes it clear that Alice's assistance was crucial to her career.

Despite the outstanding ability Althea had demonstrated, she had been kept out of the U.S. national championship matches. The U.S. Lawn Tennis Association, organizer of the official "white" tennis competitions, did not invite her to participate.

When Alice—who had opposed Nazi racism—became aware that a talented young American, on the basis of her race alone, was being denied an equal chance in her own field of tennis, she became furious. In Althea Gibson's words, Alice "kicked up a storm from one end of the tennis world to the other."

Using her respected position in that world, Alice wrote an angry letter to the USLTA's official magazine. The letter was a burning rebuke of the tennis establishment for its shameful betrayal of sportsmanship. It was also an impassioned cry for racial justice. Published in July 1950, the letter did its work. It by no means brought about racial justice in America. It didn't even end racial prejudice on the tennis court. But in August of that same year, Althea Gibson was invited to play in "the big one"—the national championships at Forest Hills. It was a square chance, which was all Althea had ever asked.

Alice's principled stand against racism, extraordinary for its time, did not win a chorus of praise. She commented later, "Some of my white so-called friends didn't like what I did. But tough."

As she grew older, Alice needed to deal with the disapproval of friends and acquaintances less often. Their views began to catch up with hers; if not, she got better at laughing at what they thought of her. Besides, she went on winning public admiration as she aged. She was looked up to as a model for a powerful new style of women's tennis. She was sought-after as a lecturer, an advisor, a teacher. She was recognized as a coach of important players—Darlene Hard,

Billie Jean King. In 1964, at fifty-one, she was inducted into the Tennis Hall of Fame; in 1967, into the International Sportsman Hall of Fame.

Before and after those years, Alice battled daunting health problems. The old damage to her lungs had re-appeared toward the end of the 1940s. She was in and out of hospitals with pneumonia. At last, the right lobe of her lung became so infected that she had to choose between having it removed or leading a completely inactive life. Given a fifty-fifty chance of surviving, she chose surgery—and got through. With her scars still healing (two ribs were also removed), she and a partner played doubles in a pro match—and won!

Nevertheless, she was frequently ill. Her doctor advised her to get away from New York's harsh climate. It was with a feeling of relief that, in 1951, she moved back to Los Angeles. There she could enjoy a warmer, sunnier climate and also be nearer her family, who still lived in San Francisco.

To her pleasure, Teach soon got in touch with her. By now, Teach was grooming a teenager named Maureen Connolly. She asked Alice to work with Maureen on her serve. In that same year, at sixteen, Maureen became the youngest victor in the history of the U.S. championships. Next, two years in a row, she won Wimbledon.

With their mutual satisfaction in Maureen's success, the rift between Alice and Teach was mended. They stayed on good terms until Teach's death, in 1963. It was a few years afterward that Brownie moved west. Alice had by then moved to Palm Desert, not far from Los Angeles, where she had a large following as a tennis teacher. To her delight, Brownie joined her there.

At seventy-three, Brownie was as cheerful and energetic as ever. She had somehow worked a late marriage into her busy life, but now was divorced. Besides her outstanding early tennis career, Brownie had been a first-class golfer in her youth. She still golfed very well and was a serious painter.

After three years, during which she and Alice happily shared a small house, Brownie went off to paint in Santa Fe, New Mexico. One weekend in 1971, when Alice was expecting her for a visit, Brownie suffered a massive stroke. She did not linger long after. Her death was a terrible blow for Alice. Brownie was more than twenty years older than Alice but had always seemed young—wise, but young. She'd been for Alice the perfect combination of sister, mother, and friend.

It was without a Brownie in her life, then, that Alice in 1981 took the news that she had colon cancer. Three surgeries followed, but that wasn't all. She had to return to the hospital for two more painful surgeries the next year.

Although Alice was never to replace Brownie—and never, as she called him in a yearning memory, in her first autobiography, "a soldier named Joe"—she went on attracting friends. Her interest in tennis was lifelong, and she found friends among the many upcoming players she admired. Personal friends included Martina Navratilova, Steffi Graf, Zina Garrison, and Gabriela Sabatini.

Among these players, she identified strongly with Martina Navratilova. The reasons seem clear in Alice's own remarks about Martina. When Alice first met the amazing new champion, in 1978, Martina was "shy and overweight." This reminded Alice of her own early self. Like Alice, too, Martina can't keep hidden behind a smooth mask her passionate attachment to the game. Win or lose, the joy of playing for its own sake—always the key to Alice's drive—is "written all over [Martina's] face."

Alice admired Martina's courage in defecting to the United States, in 1975, from Czechoslovakia's repressive rule. To this might be added Martina's honesty about her lesbianism. Alice didn't point out the similarity between Martina's qualities of courage and her own. Yet it is as striking as the likeness of their bold playing.

Alice Marble died of cancer on December 13, 1990, at the age of seventy-seven. During her last three years, she worked on her second autobiography, *Courting Danger*, co-written with journalist Dale Leatherman. Interviewed on public radio about those illness-ridden final years, Leatherman commented on Alice's hardy spirit, saying, "She never complained."

She'd come a long way from the girl who cried and threw temper tantrums when she lost a match. She'd come a long way from the young woman—and the older one—who believed she'd fall down unless her coach constantly held her up. She'd come a long way from the person who, more than once, was ready to bow out of life altogether—and later was happy that she hadn't.

Her life did not follow one steady path. In the course of it, she swung wildly from weakness to strength. Her strength—she called it "the strong me"—won out. Still, she made no secret of the fact that it waged a contest with "the weak me" all the way.

The values she cherished were simple ones. Fair play. Generosity. Honesty. Honor. The fun of playing the game as well as you can—more important than winning it. Never lording it over people—what have you got to be arrogant about, after all? They are values that she was often afraid were being lost in tennis, as she watched greed and self-display taking over. And finally: courage, which she battled to claim for herself throughout her whole life.

That is Alice Marble's main legacy. Her example has continued to inspire others, on and off the court, to follow along that hard path.

ALICE MARBLE
(1913–1990)

Outline of Life Events

September 13, 1913. Born in Beckwith, California, second youngest of five children. In **1919,** family moves to San Francisco, California. Father dies of pneumonia. Family income sinks.

1926–31. Outstanding baseball player at age thirteen. Drops baseball to focus on tennis at age fifteen. Represents Northern California Tennis Association in Northwest and Canadian championship games, **1930.** Wins Northern California junior championship, **1931.** Family scrapes together money to help send her to junior competitions in prestigious national championship games on East Coast. With no experience on grass courts used in Eastern U.S., she loses.

1931–33. At eighteen, wins Pacific Southwest Tennis Championships, becoming California's number one woman player. Attracts notice of Eleanor "Teach" Tennant, tennis coach, who gives her lessons in exchange for secretarial help. As California champion, goes East again for national championships. Playing 108 games in three days of qualifying matches, she breaks down physically, but comes away third highest ranked U.S. woman player, **1933.**

1934. Playing in Paris, France, before Wightman Cup games, collapses again. Diagnosed with tuberculosis and told she'll never play tennis again. In California sanatorium, grows weaker until Teach removes her. With routine of exercise and diet, she works with Teach for comeback. During illness, movie star Carole Lombard becomes devoted friend and supporter.

1935–1936. Begins to revolutionize women's tennis with hard-hitting "man's game." Wins singles, doubles, and mixed doubles in U.S. national championships, Forest Hills, **1936.** Ranked number one U.S. woman player (through 1940).

1937. At Wimbledon's All-England Tennis Championships, wins mixed doubles. Loses singles in semifinal of U.S. championships. After this blow and her mother's death, goes into a slump, decides to quit tennis. Consents to Teach's plea to compete in Pacific Southwest Tennis Championships. Stunning victory restores her confidence.

1938. Wins doubles and mixed doubles championships, Wimbledon. In France, has love affair with young Swiss banker Kurt Bergner, which Teach breaks up. Wins U.S. singles, doubles, and mixed doubles championships. Tries singing career. Debut at Waldorf-Astoria Hotel in New York City is well-received, but she returns to full-time tennis.

1939. Wins singles, doubles, and mixed doubles championships at Wimbledon; wins all three also at Forest Hills. World War II brings international tennis to a standstill for the next seven years.

1940. Again wins all three U.S. national championships, plus other U.S. championships. Named Woman Athlete of the Year. Co-chairs physical fitness program for Office of Civilian Defense.

1941–44. Turns professional. Plays exhibition games at U.S. military bases. U.S. enters World War II, **December 8, 1941.** Meets and marries U.S. Army Captain Joseph Crowley, **1942.** Continues professional tennis and military tours. Pregnancy ends in miscarriage after a car crash, **1944.** Soon after, on army mission, husband dies in plane crash over Germany. Alice attempts suicide. Survives but, seriously depressed, withdraws for a time from all activities.

1945–46. Recruited by U.S. Army Intelligence to spy on Kurt Bergner, former lover. Shot and wounded during espionage mission to obtain list of Nazis whose stolen treasures Bergner holds for his bank. Her photographic memory enables her to reproduce list. The war in Europe ends **May 7, 1945.** At Nuremberg International Military Tribunal **(1945– 46),** Nazis whose names Alice obtained are among those tried for war crimes. Soon after war ends, Alice breaks with Teach. Publishes autobiography, **1946.**

1950. Learns that racist policies bar African American **Althea Gibson** from access to U.S. championship games. Using her position as all-time great of women's tennis, Alice writes impassioned public letter of protest. Shortly after, **Althea** admitted to U.S. National Tennis Championships, beginning rise to international fame.

1951–52. Still suffering from early damage to lungs, survives removal of right lung, but professional tennis career ends. Moves back to California. Mends break with Teach by joining her in coaching new tennis star Maureen Connolly. Advises on Tracey-Hepburn movie *Pat and Mike*, plays bit part in the movie.

1960–80. Coaches tennis stars Billie Jean King, Darlene

Hard, many others, and teaches regularly. Inducted into Tennis Hall of Fame, **1964;** International Sportsman Hall of Fame, **1967.**

1981–1990. Survives five surgeries for colon cancer. Works on her second autobiography with journalist Dale Leatherman (published, **1991**). Dies of cancer, **December 12, 1990,** at the age of seventy-seven.

Althea Gibson

Undated photo of Althea Gibson in her early twenties. According to her own description, she'd been a cocky, ill-mannered young roughneck. She was taken in hand by black tennis enthusiasts who recognized her promise. By the time she posed for this picture, she had learned how to "be polite to everybody, and still play like a tiger and beat the liver and lights out of the ball."

Althea Gibson, during the 1980s, in her childhood neighborhood of Harlem for the kickoff of a public parks program bringing tennis to 20,000 inner city youngsters. Here, Althea shows participants the first tennis racket she used, a second-hand one given to her in 1942.

Althea Gibson in action, 1956, at the Kent Tennis Championships in Beckenham, England. This event was one of the warmup matches that took place before the All-England Championships at Wimbledon. Competing around the world and winning sixteen international championships in the month just preceding, Althea was "overtennissed" by the time she reached the Wimbledon matches. She won the Wimbledon championship the following year.

CHAPTER 1

A Harlem Girlhood

She used bad language, had bad manners, and was willing to beat up anybody who picked a fight with her. She also played hooky from school, and sometimes she stayed away from home all night. Later on, when she grew up, she didn't feel especially proud of any of that. On the other hand, she wasn't ashamed of it, either. She hadn't been a "very bad" kid, she said in her autobiography. Like others in her gang of friends, she'd been mischievous, but had stayed out of really serious trouble.

Althea Gibson was born in Silver, South Carolina, on August 25, 1927. She spent only the first three years of her life there. After that, bad harvests drove her parents, Annie and Daniel Gibson, off the tiny patch of land they farmed. They were sharecroppers; that is, they paid rent on the land by sharing their cotton crop with the landowner. It was a big share, leaving them barely enough to live on. In 1930, they earned only seventy-five dollars for the entire year's work.

Like many other poor black Southerners, the Gibsons went North, hoping for a better life. In New York City, Mr. Gibson quickly found a job as a handyman in a garage. For a few years the Gibson family stayed with Annie Gibson's sister, Sally. Then they moved into an apartment of their own in the black neighborhood of Harlem. It was there that Althea Gibson, future champion and the first African American to break the color line in tournament tennis, spent her girlhood.

■ ■ ■

Althea ducked into the shadows of a darkened building. She had glimpsed her mother just in time to hide. It was two o'clock in the morning, and Annie Gibson wasn't strolling the sidewalks for her health. She was looking for Althea. Althea had been away from home for three days, playing hooky with a girlfriend. They'd had fun. They had gone to the movies, eaten popcorn, and ridden the subway for hours, giggling at nothing in particular. At night, Althea had slept at her friend's house.

Althea suspected that a truant officer from school had visited her parents. If she went home, her father would beat the living daylights out of her. Still, she might as well return. The longer she was gone, she thought, the angrier Daddy would be. She decided to wait a while, anyway, until around six, when her father left for work. She could ride the subway some more and put off the beating until suppertime.

Twelve-year-old Althea didn't blame her father much for beating her. She faintly understood that Daniel Gibson was trying "to teach me right from wrong."

Poor Daddy must have wished there was some way he could whip me hard enough to make me behave like the other kids in the family. My brother Dan and my three sisters, Millie and Annie and Lillian, never got into any trouble at all. They were good in school, too. I was the only one who was always stepping out of line.

Hard as her father tried, his beatings didn't keep Althea out of mischief. He didn't give up, but he began teaching her how to fight him back. He gave her real boxing lessons. He knew she'd be good at it. She was tall and strong, and she had plenty of spirit. She'd never once cried when he whipped her. So he taught her to punch, jab, and block punches, and he enjoyed their workouts.

But he had other reasons for giving his oldest child boxing lessons. As Althea later said, "Harlem is a mean place to grow up in." Her father wanted "to make sure I would be able to protect myself." If that's what he wanted, he did a good job. Years before Althea became famous as a tennis player, she was known in her Harlem neighborhood as someone it was best not to pick on.

Yet she needed to defend her reputation; so she still got into fights. One that she remembers well was with a girl who sat behind her in school. The girl made a habit of yanking on Althea's pigtails. It really hurt. If Althea asked her to stop, the girl pulled harder the next time. At last, Althea told the girl to meet her after school, "and we would see just how bad she was."

In truth, Althea was scared. The girl was much bigger than she and known as a tough fighter. But with half the school there watching, Althea knew she had to go through with it.

I tried to get myself into position, so I'd have enough leverage to get off a good punch. She had just got through calling me a pig-tailed bitch when I . . . brought my right hand all the way up from the floor and smashed her right in the face with all my might. I hit her so hard she just fell like a lump. Honest to God, she was out cold. Everybody backed away from me and just stared at me, and I turned around like I was Joe Louis and walked on home.

Althea also fought boys, if she needed to, and once she punched a man other than her father, an uncle. He was slapping his wife's face when Althea walked in on a quarrel between them. "Little lady Robin Hood . . . I sashayed right up to him and punched him in the jaw," Althea recalled. She knocked him down, yelling at him to leave his wife alone. "I was lucky," she adds, "he didn't get up and knock all my teeth out."

Besides playing hooky and getting into fights, Althea did some petty thieving with her friends. They took only food—popsicles and dixie cups from the corner grocery, vegetables and fruits from boxcars or outdoor stands. They loved to snatch a yam and roast it over a fire in a vacant lot. "Now I realize how poor we were, and how little we had," Althea says. But it didn't seem bad at the time. She never felt sorry for herself.

Althea believes she didn't get into big trouble mostly because she and her girlfriends didn't join any of Harlem's "so-called social clubs."

We didn't care for all the drinking and narcotics and sex that they went in for in those clubs—and we didn't care for the stickups that they turned to sooner or later in order to get money for the things they were doing. I didn't like to go to school but I had no interest in going to jail, either.

More than anything, Althea loved to play games that required skill with a ball. She didn't care if it was bowling, baseball, or paddle tennis, although basketball was her favorite. That was mainly why she skipped school. "I couldn't see any point in wasting all that time that I could be spending shooting baskets."

Althea played at the park, or at the school gymnasium at night. There wasn't much open space in Harlem for games of any kind, however. To ease the problem, the city of New

York blocked certain Harlem streets to traffic in the day-time. The city then hired adults to act as play leaders for these black "play streets."

The Gibson family happened to live on one of the play streets that was set up for paddle tennis. Paddle tennis is a little like tennis, but played with wooden paddles and on a smaller court. Getting the hang of it quickly, Althea was soon paddle tennis champion of her block. Representing her block, she won medals in contests with other Harlem play streets.

The year that Althea was thirteen, a Harlem band leader named Buddy Walker took a summer job as a play street leader. He was very impressed with Althea's skill, and one day he had an inspiration. Given a chance, he thought, this fine athlete might be able to play real tennis as well as she played paddle tennis.

He talked over his idea with Althea, who said, "Sure, why not?" Buddy bought her two secondhand tennis rackets at five dollars each. At the handball court in a park nearby, he watched Althea hit tennis balls against the wall. He "got very excited about how well I hit the ball," Althea recalled.

A few days later, Buddy Walker took Althea to the Harlem River Tennis Courts. He'd asked a friend to play a couple of sets of tennis with Althea there. Althea, who loved to com-pete in any sport, immediately loved tennis. She played so well that quite a few other players simply stopped their games to watch.

Among these watchers was a black schoolteacher, Juan Serrell. He told Althea and Buddy that he'd like to arrange for Althea to play at the Cosmopolitan Tennis Club, of which he was a member. He could set it up so that Althea played with the club's professional tennis teacher—and let other club members see her in action.

Now Buddy was really excited. The Cosmopolitan Club

was at the very top among New York's black private clubs. Its members, from the highest rungs of black society, had as much influence as African Americans could have in the white world.

That influence wasn't much in tennis, however. All the important tennis tournaments in the country were sponsored by white tennis clubs. Black people weren't allowed to play at these clubs, and thus were kept from competing in the major tournaments.

Over the years, black country clubs—such as the Cosmopolitan Club—had formed their own national tennis association. This was the American Tennis Association, or ATA. It served the same purpose in the black tennis world as the U.S. Lawn Tennis Association (USLTA) served in the white. It made and enforced the rules that governed black tennis events and players.

As long as no black player was allowed to compete in the major tennis tournaments, black players could never show that they had skills equal to those of white players. The ATA and its member clubs were therefore always on the lookout for a player outstanding enough to break the color barrier.

When Althea performed at the Cosmopolitan Club, hope stirred among the watching members. It also stirred in the club's professional, Fred Johnson, with whom she played. Her gracefulness, the natural talent she brought to the game, were plain to all. The small crowd decided to take up a collection to buy Althea a junior membership in the club. That way, she could play regularly on a good court and take lessons from Mr. Johnson. That was exactly what Juan Serrell and Buddy Walker had wanted.

Althea was pleased, too, even though, as she later wrote, she knew she wasn't "the tennis type." She didn't mean that she wasn't suited to playing tennis itself. She meant that she wasn't the kind of "fine lady" a tennis player was supposed to be. Like young Alice Marble when she began to play tennis, Althea had no use for the super-polite manners expected on the court. She got angry when she was losing, and she would just as soon have punched out an opponent. And yet—also like Alice—Althea liked dressing up in the "pretty white tennis clothes." They looked good on her straight, long-limbed ebony figure. Gradually, she began to like the polite manners, too—although it was going to be a while before she learned to use them.

I began to understand that you could walk out on the court like a lady, all dressed up in immaculate white, be polite to everybody, and still play like a tiger and beat the liver and lights out of the ball.

Meanwhile, at home, her father often still beat the liver and lights out of Althea. She wanted to escape his punishments—and thought she saw a way. From a girlfriend who had been abused by both her parents, Althea learned about the Society for the Prevention of Cruelty to Children. The SPCC "would take in kids who were in trouble and had no place to go."

The SPCC took Althea in—but it also notified her parents. Her daddy came to get her. Although she swore she'd never run away again, he beat her with a strap. This time, she showed the SPCC people the red welts on her back. They said they wouldn't release her to her father unless she wanted to go.

Althea enjoyed what she called the "country club" life at the SPCC. The meals were good, and she had a comfortable bed in the dormitory. She didn't mind the bit of work she had to do, helping to keep the dorm scrubbed clean. By now, Althea had somehow managed to pass from junior to senior high school. Because of her poor grades, she was sent to a trade school. For a while, she attended regularly, because she liked the sewing classes. However, most of her girlfriends had gone to regular high school, and she was soon bored.

Restless at the dorm, too, after a while she returned home. The school authorities made a deal with her: they would let her take a job, as long as she went to night school. For a time she had jobs on and off—and nobody seemed to notice when she stopped night classes. She sometimes lived at home and sometimes in a room "the Welfare ladies" rented for her. Nights, she played basketball and bummed around with girlfriends.

She knew that her backers in the Cosmopolitan Club would have been deeply shocked by the "wild" life she led. The club members, struggling to disprove racist stereotypes of black people as "shiftless" and "loose," made a point of correct living. For the moment, Althea figured that what they didn't know wouldn't hurt them—as long as she worked hard at her tennis. And since it was such joy to learn the game better and better, she worked very hard.

Her interest took a great leap forward on the never-to-be-forgotten day when she first watched Alice Marble. Marble was playing an exhibition match at the Cosmopolitan Club.

I can still remember saying to myself, boy, would I like to be able to play tennis like that! She was the only woman tennis player I'd ever seen that I felt exactly that way about. Until I saw her I'd always had eyes only for the good men players . . . Watching her . . . I saw possibilities in the game of tennis that I had never seen.

She had a chance to test her own abilities in her very first tournament, in the summer of 1942. The occasion was the

New York State Open Championship sponsored by the American Tennis Association. Her coach, Fred Johnson, entered her in the girls' singles of this event, held at the Cosmopolitan Club. When Althea won the championship, she was a little surprised—"but not much. By this time I was accustomed to winning games." Her cocky attitude bothered some club members. They couldn't see, Althea said later, that being assertive and a show-off was part of her defense against hurt or disappointment.

Later that summer, the club sent Althea to the ATA national girls' championship at Lincoln University, an all-black school in Pennsylvania. There she got all the way to the finals before being defeated. She had come a long way from paddle tennis.

Her manners, however, still had a way to go. The woman who defeated her recalled, "After I beat [Althea], she headed straight for the grandstand without bothering to shake hands. Some kid had been laughing at her and she was going to throw him out."

But as new people entered Althea's life, she began slowly to change. A club member named Rhoda Smith said, "Althea had played in the street all her life and she just didn't know any better." Rhoda Smith befriended her, buying her tennis clothes, teaching her manners. Althea was more polished by the time she won the ATA's national girls' championship in both 1944 and 1945.

In 1945, at eighteen, Althea was free to run her own life. She took a job as a waitress and rented a room in the family home of a new friend, Gloria Nightingale. It was Gloria who, one night at a bowling alley, introduced Althea to Sugar Ray Robinson. This young black man—already on his way to becoming a great world boxing champion—was famous, especially in Harlem.

With her usual boldness, Althea said, "So you're Sugar

Ray Robinson? Well, I can beat you bowling!" Sugar Ray liked this tall, spunky kid right away, and so did his young wife, Edna Mae. They welcomed her into their lives and gave her warmth and attention. Because she longed to learn to play a saxophone, they bought her a good secondhand one. Above all, they urged her to better herself through her athletic gifts.

In 1946, Althea was old enough to play in the ATA national women's championships. The ATA paid her expenses for the trip to all-black Wilberforce College in Ohio. There, Althea made it to the singles final before losing. The winner was an older, more experienced player, but some of Althea's sponsors blamed her cocky attitude. (She admitted she'd been overconfident.)

But Althea's playing impressed two black physicians who were watching. Dr. Hubert A. Eaton and Dr. Robert W. Johnson were interested in promoting black tennis talent. They told Althea they'd be glad to help her find a college scholarship. That way, they said, she could get an education and improve her tennis at the same time.

"That would be great," Althea replied. "Except I never even been to high school."

It was the last thing the two doctors expected. But it didn't stop them long. Althea was just too promising to pass up.

CHAPTER 2

"To Be Somebody—If It Killed Me"

Dr. Eaton and Dr. Johnson presented an idea that took
Althea's breath away. They proposed that during the school
year, Althea would live in Wilmington, North Carolina.
There, she'd stay with Dr. Eaton and his family, go to the
local high school, and practice tennis with the doctor on his
private court. Summers, she'd live in Lynchburg, Virginia,
with Dr. Johnson's family, and travel with him to ATA tournaments. Each doctor would pay for Althea's living expenses
while she was with his family. They had talked over this idea
with the ATA officials, who thought it seemed fine.

Althea understood how generous their offer was. But—
the *South*? The South, she'd heard, was a terrible place for
black people. They couldn't drink from public fountains or
use public toilets except those marked "colored." They were
permitted to sit only at the back of buses and street
cars. They could be arrested, tried, and convicted, for no
reason at all. They could be lynched—even children—and
their murderers never punished.

Althea didn't share her daddy's occasional dreams, in
crowded Harlem, of open land and trees. She'd formed a
notion of the hopeless economic conditions that had forced
him North to begin with. She didn't have her mother's few
happy girlhood memories of outdoor country living, either. Like Althea, Annie Gibson was "no delicate flower." She
had worked hard and played hard, and had loved riding
horses—even mules and cows. None of that appealed to

Althea, a city girl. She knew "up North . . . wasn't heaven" for black folk, but it felt safe to her.

It was Edna Mae and Sugar Ray Robinson who talked Althea into leaving. "No matter what you want to do, tennis or music or what, you'll be better at it if you get some education," Sugar Ray said. Althea idolized Sugar Ray—not only because he'd been kind to her, but because "he was somebody." Althea had always wanted to be somebody, too. If she acted overconfident, it was often out of fear that maybe she didn't really amount to much.

So she made up her mind to brave the terrors of the South, to take this chance "to be somebody—if it killed me."

In September 1946, with a ticket sent by Dr. Eaton, Althea boarded a train. The following day she arrived at Wilmington, carrying in each hand a shabby cardboard suitcase. The suitcases were tied with belts to keep them from falling open. She wore a cheap cotton dress, badly wrinkled from the night she'd spent on the train. From a strap around her neck hung her saxophone. "I must have been a sight to behold," she later wrote.

The black chauffeur who met her with Dr. Eaton's big car didn't seem to see anything odd about her. Neither did Mrs. Eaton. She hugged and kissed Althea, then showed her to her room. It was a beautiful room, Althea thought, like the entire beautiful house. Because Althea hadn't had breakfast, Mrs. Eaton said she should help herself to anything in the kitchen that looked good to her. Althea met the Eaton children, who greeted her with friendly chatter. By the time Dr. Eaton came home, Althea had stopped being worried that the family wouldn't like her. She and Dr. Eaton went out to the handsome backyard tennis court, where they played until dinnertime.

At nineteen, Althea only had enough school credits for the seventh grade. She did well enough on aptitude tests to be placed as a high school sophomore. However, it was understood that unless she kept up with her studies she'd have to go to a lower grade. Althea badly wanted to earn her diploma in three years. "I buckled down to my schoolwork like nobody's business."

She made an effort, too, to fit in at Williston Industrial High School, the high school "for colored." She joined the girls' basketball team, the choir, and the band. Not surprisingly, she was soon the basketball team's star, and in time was elected captain. A good saxophone player, she was welcome in the band. On the other hand, in the choir, her deep voice sounded strange among the girls. The choir leader placed her with the tenor boys. This made the girls giggle, so Althea quit.

In general, the girls weren't friendly to Althea, even though she tried to fit in with them, too. She had her hair styled once or twice at a beauty parlor. Although she preferred pants, she wore the dresses Mrs. Eaton bought for her. Tall (nearly five feet ten) and graceful, Althea could have been a model in her new dresses. Her face was radiant when she smiled. Yet the Williston girls looked at her "like I was a freak." She reacted by showing off on the football and baseball fields, practicing with the boys' varsity teams. That made the girls laugh at her even more.

Althea's feelings were so hurt, she almost hated the girls. She had less trouble with the boys. In the band, she made friends with a group that had formed a small jazz combo, and they soon asked her to join. She sang and played sax with them at their gigs around town. Sometimes she dated the trumpet player.

Mainly, she studied and played tennis—with many partners. All the area's black tennis players came to Dr. Eaton's court. They weren't allowed to play on any public court in Wilmington. A number of white players were also regulars.

They were people who didn't want the law to tell them how to choose their company. They liked Dr. Eaton, and they didn't approve of segregation.

Both Dr. Eaton and Dr. Johnson were more respected among whites than blacks usually were in the South—as well as better-off. Each was a surgeon as well as a physician, with his own clinic, to which black patients flocked. Many Southern hospitals at that time admitted few black patients, except in extreme emergencies. White physicians, if they tended black patients at all, had separate waiting areas. And some black people, given a choice, didn't want a white physician.

Althea never got used to the way black people were treated in the South. She was outraged every time she had to sit in the back of a bus. It made her furious that although her dime was taken at a lunch counter, she couldn't eat her hot dog there, but had to eat it in the street. Although she loved the movies, she didn't enjoy them in the South, because she couldn't choose her own seat. Black people had to sit in the balcony. She felt "ashamed in a way I'd never been ashamed back in New York."

> **It wasn't a Ku Klux Klan nightmare like I'd been afraid it might be. I managed to conform. . . . But I . . . made up my mind . . . that I was never going to live any place in the South, at least not while those laws were in existence.**

It was also hard for Althea, in quite a different way, to conform to the Eatons' orderly family life. She was treated just like the other children, even getting the same weekly allowance. But she was also expected to follow the same rules. Everyone in the Eaton family sat down to meals on time. Nobody bummed around all night. In Harlem, Althea had done as she pleased for a long time, and "sometimes, naturally, I felt like rebelling."

One night, she did rebel. Dr. and Mrs. Eaton had gone out with Dr. Eaton's mother, whose car was parked in the driveway. Althea, taught to drive by the Robinsons, gave way to an impulse. She grabbed the keys from the hall table, drove to the home of her friend the trumpet player, and took him for a quick spin. She returned before the Eatons, but not before a friend of the Eatons saw her—and then told on her.

When the doctor faced Althea the next day, he was furious. She didn't try to lie about it. She apologized, terrified that he would send her away. Perhaps he considered it, but then decided to give her another chance. He never said another word about the matter—and Althea didn't test her good luck further.

At vacation time, Althea left for Dr. Johnson's home in Lynchburg. Althea came to adore "my two doctors," as she referred to them in the dedication of her first book. They were, she said, very much alike and yet quite different. They were both devoted family men, both ardent players of tennis and poker. Dr. Eaton, tall and slim, was interested in photography. He was far quieter than short, husky Dr. Johnson, who'd been a university football star.

Dr. Johnson's nickname was Whirlwind—and Althea's summers became whirlwinds set in motion by the doctor. He had a team of five or six players, including his son, all of them male except Althea. They spent the early summer practicing on Dr. Johnson's backyard court. Then they took off for a round of tournaments, their rackets, bags, and bodies stuffed into Dr. Johnson's big Buick.

Althea never forgot her first tour, in 1947. It started with contests in Washington, D.C., Philadelphia, New York, and New Jersey. Then the bunch set out for Kentucky, stopping off first to play a tournament in Kansas City, Missouri. There, it was so broiling hot, one team member fainted in mid-match. Near their destination, Louisville, Kentucky, they had a flat tire. Just then, a rainstorm struck. Unable to fix the tire, all six of them spent the night trying to sleep inside the car—in layers.

Dr. Johnson had wisely flown ahead from Kansas City. He greeted his team with a heartless grin. "Have a nice trip?"

That summer, Dr. Johnson and Althea won the mixed doubles title in eight out of nine tournaments. Althea won the championship in every one of the nine singles tournaments she played. The most important of these was the ATA national women's singles championship, which she took 6–3, 6–0. Dr. Eaton attended that one. "Both doctors were mighty pleased."

Althea won the ATA title the next summer, and the one after that. (She was to win it ten straight years, until she stopped, "to give somebody else a chance.") In 1949, "For whatever it was worth, I was the best woman player in Negro tennis."

The ATA didn't think it was enough. Its leaders knew that race relations in the country were changing, if slowly. Up until then, only white players had competed in the nation's major tennis tournaments, controlled by the U.S. Lawn Tennis Association (USLTA). The USLTA could defend itself against charges of racism, if need be, on the ground that there were no top-class players who were not white. But what if a highly qualified black player should come upon the scene?

The leaders of the ATA believed that Althea was that player. As Althea put it, the ATA hadn't wanted "to kick up a fuss" until it was sure it had a really outstanding player. Althea had shown herself a superior player, over and over. The ATA leaders thought the time had come to make a fuss.

There wasn't much fuss, at first, because the USLTA did

yield a bit to the ATA. Althea believed that the USLTA gave way because of a basic decency in tennis people. "Maybe some of them were reluctant to see it happen, but most of them were men and women of good will." However that may be, USLTA and ATA officials met for a quiet and apparently reasonable talk. Not long after, the ATA received word that if Althea Gibson sent in an entry form for the Eastern Indoor Championships, she would be accepted.

Indoor tennis, played in a big, public place rather than at a country club, didn't have the snob appeal and prestige of outdoor tennis. But it was a huge step forward for a black player to be included in any important "white" competition. The ATA people were very excited. Althea was especially pleased that the contest was to be held at the 143rd Street armory, in Harlem. She knew those courts well. She also played well, winning her first two matches. She got as far as the quarterfinals before she was defeated 8–6, 6–0.

The USLTA was impressed with Althea's playing. She was now invited to stay another week, to play in its National Indoor Championships. She was making just the sort of progress the ATA had hoped for. Two years before, a black physician, Reginald Weir, had competed in the indoor championships. But he had not done well and the USLTA hadn't invited him to later tournaments. Both the ATA and Althea felt that she was getting a fair chance.

The USLTA events were Althea's first experiences as the only black player in an all-white event. As might be expected, she was tense, but she was pleasantly surprised by the behavior of the other women players. "It wasn't just that they were polite; they were genuinely friendly," said Althea. "It was as though they realized how much of a strain I was under, and they wanted to do whatever they could to help."

Once again, Althea did well, winning her first and second matches before losing in the quarterfinal. The ATA was happy with her showing and so was Althea. Together with the ready friendliness of the white women tournament players, this experience gave her "a lot of hope for the future."

Back in Wilmington, she found further hope, reaching the goal she'd set herself there. By working hard, she finished high school in three years. Better yet, to her surprise, she graduated tenth in her class.

It was 1949, and Althea was twenty-one. Among the black colleges she'd applied to, a number wrote back with keen interest. She chose Florida A & M University, in Tallahassee, Florida. The school offered her a full scholarship, all expenses paid. Further, she was invited to go right away, to spend the summer playing tennis on the campus before classes started.

Althea had become very attached to the Eaton and Johnson families. She well understood how much they'd done for her. At the same time, she was fully adult now and eager to feel more independent.

Two days after graduation, she packed her bags and left for Tallahassee.

CHAPTER 3

Ups and Downs

Even if Althea had wanted to get into trouble—and she didn't—there wasn't much to get into at Florida A & M. The campus was green and beautiful. She went to her classes, studied, and played a lot of tennis. And that was about it. Her life, like that of all Florida A & M students, was strictly regulated. Seniors could stay out until eleven o'clock at night. Other students had to be in by nine. Before leaving the campus, students had to sign out, stating where they were going.

There weren't many places students could go, anyway. Either the college stopped them, or segregation did. The college allowed them to visit only one off-campus café. They could get a beer there, at certain hours. At the campus canteen they could get soft drinks and hamburgers, shoot pool, and play cards. Only one Tallahassee theater admitted blacks, but it never showed the latest movies. They could see better movies at the campus auditorium. Sometimes dances were held in the gym.

Althea cared less about campus social life than other students did. Having turned twenty-two in August, she was older than most of them. She could complain, as they did, about signing in and out. She could groan with them about having to dress up three times a week for chapel. She even pledged a sorority, Alpha Kappa Alpha. But mostly, she said, she thought of herself as "a sort of aunt to the other kids." She was amused when she was chosen to head the student committee that disciplined those who broke college rules. "Wild" Althea!

College didn't distract Althea from her keen wish to climb to higher levels in the "white" tennis world. At the beginning of 1950, she was invited to New York to play for the second time in the Eastern Indoor Championships. This time, she won the championship, going on to play in the National Indoors again. There, she got to the finals before being defeated.

Althea's college welcomed her back with banners and a marching band. Everyone knew that she had won a great victory by getting to the finals. Had she been white, the next step would have come as a matter of course. She would have been invited to the summer Eastern outdoor tournaments. These were held by member clubs of the USLTA. They were played on the grass courts of private Eastern tennis clubs in such places as Seabright and South Orange, New Jersey, and East Hampton, New York. Players who did well in those tournaments were invited to play in the national championships at Forest Hills, New York City. That tournament, the most important in the U.S. tennis world, was what Althea was aiming for.

However, as spring turned to summer, no invitations came. "The USLTA acted as if I wasn't there." But if the USLTA wanted to pretend that Althea didn't exist, tennis fans knew that she did. White sports writers for major newspapers started to raise questions. Was Althea Gibson going to play at Forest Hills, or wasn't she? It was understood that she wouldn't be invited to play there until she had proven herself in some grass court tournaments. "But," as Althea later wrote, "the newspapers began to ask, if I wasn't given a chance to play, how could I ever prove myself?" She added: "The trouble was, nobody at Seabright, East Hampton, Newport, or in the offices of the USLTA seemed to be listening."

The deeper trouble was that the USLTA's member clubs were as racist as their parent organization. They didn't want to open their doors—thereby opening tournament tennis itself—to African-American players. It was one thing for major league baseball, in 1947, to admit the brilliant black player Jackie Robinson. Baseball, after all, was for "the masses." Tennis, on the other hand, was the sport of "ladies and gentlemen."

Or was it? Would ladies and gentlemen be so *ungentle* as to deny a promising player a fair chance to show what she could do? This question was now asked, clearly, and publicly, by one of the greatest players in tennis history. She had the admiration and respect of thousands, including Althea. She was Alice Marble.

Alice Marble made her position known in the official journal of the USLTA, *American Lawn Tennis*. In its July 1950 issue, she wrote an impassioned plea—not so much for Althea Gibson as for racial justice. It read, in part:

> If tennis is a sport for ladies and gentlemen, it's also time we acted a little more like gentle people and less like sanctimonious hypocrites. If there is anything left in the name of sportsmanship, it's more than time to display what it means to us. If Althea Gibson represents a challenge to the present crop of women players, it's only fair that they should meet that challenge. . . .
>
> I can't honestly say that I believe Miss Gibson to be a potential champion; I don't know. In the [National Indoors Championships] there were moments when she exhibited a bold, exciting game that will doubtlessly improve against first-class competition. But if she is refused a chance to succeed or to fail, then there is an uneradicable mark against a game to

which I have devoted most of my life, and I would be bitterly ashamed. . . .

She is not being judged by the yardstick of ability but by . . . her pigmentation. . . .

If the field of sports has got to pave the way for all of civilization, let's do it. . . . The entrance of Negroes into national tennis is as inevitable as it has proven to be in baseball, in football, or in boxing; there is no denying so much talent. . . . Eventually the tennis world will rise up en masse to protest the injustices. . . . Eventually—why not now?

In her autobiography, Althea quoted the article in full. She commented: "It kicked up a storm from one end of the tennis world to the other." Alice Marble later recalled, "Some of my white so-called friends didn't like what I did. But tough."

The white tennis world was at first stunned—and then ashamed. "All of a sudden," Althea wrote, "the dam broke." The Orange Lawn Tennis Club, in New Jersey, invited her to play in the Eastern Grass Court Championships. This was a major tournament. Althea made it through to the second round. After that, she was admitted to the National Clay Courts Championships in Chicago. There, she got to the quarterfinals before losing 6–2, 6–3. These two events qualified her to compete for the U.S. championships—if the USLTA was willing now to admit her.

It was. In August, the big news came. The USLTA announced that she was one of fifty-two women who had been accepted to play in the national championships at Forest Hills. The USLTA president said matter-of-factly—as if he didn't hear the historic crash as the color bar came down in tournament tennis: "Miss Gibson has been accepted on her ability."

Miss Gibson said simply, "That was all I had ever asked." She was aware that many people—particularly those of her own race—saw her every victory as a step forward for African Americans. Althea herself took a slightly different view:

> I have never regarded myself as a crusader. I try to do the best I can in every situation I find myself in, and naturally I'm always glad when something I do turns out to be helpful and important to all Negroes. . . . But I don't consciously beat the drums for any special cause, not even the cause of the Negro in the United States, because I feel that our best chance to advance is to prove ourselves as individuals. . . . This doesn't mean that I'm opposed to the fight for integration of the schools or other movements like that. It simply means that in my own career I try to steer clear of political involvements and make my way as Althea Gibson, private individual. I feel that if I am a worthy person, and if I have something worth while to contribute, I will be accepted on my own merits. . . .

Althea must have known that her "merits" weren't the only issue for the USLTA. In fact, later in life, she proved her concern for all who suffer unequal odds in sport. Yet in her own career, she blamed herself alone for failures or disappointments.

At the moment, Althea Gibson, "private individual," was nervous about playing at Forest Hills. Among other things, she'd never laid eyes on the big West Side Tennis Club in Forest Hills, where the nationals were played. She wanted to know the layout—how the courts and the stands were placed, where the dressing rooms were, and so on. Although they had never met, she phoned Sarah Palfrey Cooke for her help. Sarah, a white player and a former U.S. champion, agreed at once. She arranged to tour the club with Althea, and to practice there with her.

The practice session with Sarah—a marvelous player—did a lot to calm Althea. It was a comfort, too, to be the house guest of Rhoda Smith, who had taken Althea in hand some years before at the Cosmopolitian Club. On the first day of the nationals, Rhoda and Althea rode the subway from Rhoda's home in Harlem to the West Side Tennis Club. Althea had scarcely changed into her tennis clothes before a throng of reporters and photographers crowded in on her. Because no black person had ever before played at Forest Hills, Althea's presence was a big event in sports news. Unprepared for the attention, Althea again became nervous. She was grateful that Rhoda was with her.

In spite of her nerves, Althea easily won the first match. Then she had to face the sports reporters all over again. At last, she escaped with Rhoda for a quiet dinner. After scanning the newspapers, she went to bed early.

Some news writers complained that the managers of the tournament had discriminated against Althea. That was because Althea was given the court with the smallest seating capacity, farthest from the clubhouse. Meanwhile, film star Ginger Rogers—understood not to be a genuine contender for the title—played her doubles match in front of the clubhouse before a huge crowd. Althea refused to be upset. She later noted humorously: "Ginger Rogers was a far greater attraction . . . than Althea Gibson. I would have been far more interested in her myself."

This incident shows the way Althea sometimes used her sense of humor to bypass political conflict. Humor may also have been her way of overcoming feelings of hatred or bitterness. If so, it helped her survive with exceptional grace and goodwill.

The second day at Forest Hills was the big event for Althea. She faced Louise Brough, who was not only a former U.S. champion, but also three-time winner of the famous All-England Championships. As promised, Alice Marble was there—"rooting my heart out," as she said, for Althea. Walking to the courts with a smiling Alice, Althea smiled bravely, too. But she felt scared to death.

Her tension lasted through the first set, which she lost 6–1. But in the second set, she loosened up. She won it 6–3. By the third set, Althea "got hot." She pulled ahead to a 7–6 lead. "Rarely since Alice Marble's championship reign has a woman shown so much stroking power as she did," ran one newspaper account. Louise Brough began to look flustered. "Everyone in the stands," continued the account, "sensed that a fabulous upset was in the making."

Few spectators had noticed that the skies were darkening. Now they opened, and a violent thunderstorm struck. The match had to be called off until the following day.

The delay gave Louise a chance to recover from her shock and to regain confidence. Althea, on the other hand, had an entire evening and the next morning in which to worry. By the time play resumed the next day, she reported, "I was a nervous wreck."

All the same, she put up a terrific fight before Louise took the match. Most observers believed that, if not for the storm, Althea would have walked off with victory. "The courage and the power of this unknown colored girl" were noted in a dramatic account that appeared in the New York *Journal-American*.

USLTA officials were, of course, impressed. Before Althea returned to college, one of them met with her and an ATA representative. They talked about Althea's playing at Wimbledon in spring 1951. The USLTA offered to arrange for her to be coached, before Wimbledon, by a top-flight tennis teacher who lived in Michigan.

Now Althea began a busy sophomore year at college. Besides her studies, she held a paying job as assistant to the head of the women's physical education department. In March, she went down to Miami to play in the Good Neighbor Tournament. She was the first black player ever invited to compete in an otherwise all-white tournament in the Deep South.

But soon she was to break the color barrier at a far more important tennis event: the All-England Tennis Championships at Wimbledon. This international event was the best-known and most respected tennis tournament in the world. It was considered a great honor to be invited to play there.

So, in May, when Althea flew to Detroit, Michigan, to meet her USLTA-chosen coach, she found herself a celebrity. At her hotel, the manager told her that Joe Louis, then world heavyweight boxing champion, had said that she was to use his personal suite. Joe Louis wasn't the only black resident of Detroit looking out for Althea. A group of black citizens raised funds by putting on a variety show. The proceeds of $770 were for Althea's use for hotels, meals, and spending money on her trip.

Joe Louis presented Althea with a round-trip airplane ticket to London. Although the ATA had already purchased her ticket, Althea—whose salary was forty dollars a month—was delighted to have two tickets. She cashed in the ATA's and handed its secretary the money, to bank for her. "I was flush!" she recalled.

At Wimbledon, her gaiety melted. From the start, she felt uneasy. Instead of being placed far away from the main action, as she'd been at Forest Hills, she played her first set on Centre Court. It was the court in front of the box of the royal family of England, usually assigned to important players—which Althea knew she wasn't. Rarely suspicious, she wondered "if I was put on Centre Court either to show me off or to see me get beaten."

She wasn't beaten then, but in the third round she took a walloping. After so much hoopla, it was over.

She had hoped to make a better showing, even if she hadn't expected to win the championship on her first try. She didn't have the heart, now, to do much sightseeing in England. Her flight back to the United States was sad, filled with regrets.

Not everyone shared her gloomy view. After all, she had made it as far as the Wimbledon quarterfinals. In 1952, she was invited to nearly all the big Eastern tournaments. That year, she was ranked the ninth-best U.S. woman player. She moved up to number seven in 1953.

In the same year, she graduated from Florida A & M. She felt proud and happy. Above all, she was grateful to those who had pushed her onward. Offered a job as a physical education instructor at Lincoln University, she accepted. Lincoln was a black school in Jefferson City, Missouri. Her salary was $2800 a year—good pay for a beginning college instructor at that time.

Meanwhile, rain began to patter on the bright parade of Althea Gibson's tennis career. True, she went on winning the yearly ATA tournament. But in the more important world of the USLTA competitions, she did not progress. In 1954, her national ranking slipped from number seven to number thirteen. Her appearances at Forest Hills no longer caused a sensation. Worse, in 1954, she didn't last beyond the first round. The popular black magazine *Jet* labeled her "The Biggest Disappointment in Tennis."

But not everyone gave up on Althea's career. About this time, a longtime tennis acquaintance told her he'd like to coach her. He was Sydney Llewellyn, a black Harlem cab driver and a gifted part-time tennis teacher. He still believed that Althea could make it to the top. Just as most other experts were forgetting about her, Sydney began to work with her in the summers. He taught her a new grip and a more limber stroke. He spent hours teaching her his own theory on court strategy. She saw her game starting to improve.

Always an optimist, Althea worked hard with Sydney. There were plenty of good things in her life, she thought. She had a job, and her parents were proud of her. She had good friends—Dr. Eaton and Dr. Johnson and their families, Sugar Ray and Edna Mae Robinson, and another family, the Darbens, whom she'd met through the ATA and often visited in the East, and various musicians and tennis players. She was lucky, she thought, to have so much.

Besides all that, she was in love.

CHAPTER 4

A Wider World

In her autobiography, Althea does not name the man she fell in love with at Lincoln University. She calls him simply "my captain." A black U.S. Army officer, he was in charge of the university's Reserve Officers' Training Corps (ROTC).

Twenty-six-year-old Althea hadn't been in love before. She had dated a few men since the trumpet player in Wilmington. One of them, William Darben, had asked her to marry him. Althea was fond of Will, as she was of the whole Darben family. When tennis matches brought her to the East, she stayed in their home in New Jersey and shared a room with Rosemary, one of three Darben sisters. But liking Will and his family wasn't the same as loving him. Although she went on dating him, he remained just a good friend.

With the captain, it was different. He was a good friend, too—but he was more. Althea had never felt this way about anyone before. "Being in love, and being loved by somebody, was something brand new to me," she wrote.

Until her love affair with the captain, Althea thought of herself as pretty sharp and as older than her age. After all, she'd been a child of the streets and had knocked around a lot since. But the captain, fifteen years older than she, well-traveled and worldly, made her aware of how little she really knew about life. Certainly, she wasn't experienced in love. She didn't know that it could change your whole view of living and of what you wanted for yourself.

Althea and the captain saw a lot of each other. The more they did, the more they liked being together. Little by little, Althea's longings for a certain kind of future began to change.

> **It's funny, but the things that have seemed most important to you can suddenly become very unimportant compared with being with, and pleasing, somebody you love. Tennis no longer seemed like everything in the world to me. . . . If the man in question had been closer to my own age . . . maybe I really might have given up tournament tennis altogether.**

At this point, her tennis career didn't seem to be going anywhere, anyway. Althea herself summed it up coldly: "I was champion of nothing but the ATA." The one person who still seemed to believe strongly in her tennis future was her coach, Sydney Llewellyn. It was he who had kept alive in her some hope for such a future. She would hate to disappoint Sydney by letting go of that hope.

Yet Althea felt something had to be done about her future, quite apart from tennis or the captain. When she'd landed a job at Lincoln, she was at first relieved that she didn't have to live on handouts anymore. As her second year of teaching began, however, and her yearly salary rose only to $3000, she felt discouraged. She was paying $48.50 a month for rent and making payments on a secondhand automobile. Her pay—as high as that of many beginning white college teachers then—would get her by. But she wanted more than to "get by." She wanted to put aside something for the future. She wanted to help her family. She wanted to live better herself.

"I'm tired of never having any *real* money," Althea said.

The captain told Althea, "There's a good career waiting for you in the Women's Army Corps, if you want it."

They were sitting over cups of coffee at the university canteen. In Jefferson City, as in Tallahassee, there weren't many places where black people were welcome. "As a college graduate," the captain went on, "you can enter the WACs as an officer. You can get a good salary, and retirement with a pension." He put his head to one side, smiling at her. "You'd look snazzy in the uniform. Anyway, think about it."

Althea did think about it—more and more as the school year went forward. Besides being discontent with her salary, it was hard for her to put up with Jefferson City. She'd expected it to be free of the hateful segregation practices of the Deep South, but that wasn't the case. Off-campus, because of her race, she was barred from nearly all recreation. Even the bowling alleys were off-limits, because whites objected to black customers.

Althea felt cooped up or angry a lot of the time. When she wasn't with her captain, she found release in sports. In addition to tennis, she pitched and played the outfield for the faculty softball team. She had to do without basketball; the men who made up the faculty team said they didn't want her to get hurt. Their explanation was questionable, as they'd seen Althea in action. Some years later, the head of the Physical Education Department told a reporter:

> You had to look two or three times at Althea to convince yourself that she was a girl. She played all the games so well. You couldn't tell she was a girl by the way she pitched or the way she shagged fly balls in the outfield.

It seems likely that the faculty men were practicing their

own form of discrimination against Althea—as a woman. Ideas of what women should and shouldn't do were rigid in the 1950s. Black or white, women had narrower limits than men. Althea, although she excelled in the "male" field of competitive sport, had limits, too. Some, she accepted. In her autobiography, she made it clear that she hesitated to marry the captain because she didn't want to give up tournament tennis. It didn't seem to occur to her, at that time, to marry *and* pursue tennis seriously. Unlike men, women were expected to choose between marriage and the demands of a career.

Even at this low point in her tennis career, Althea wasn't ready to choose. As for her captain, he had his own reason for hesitating: he thought he was too old for Althea. After a time, they decided that they would simply be friends. When the school year ended and they parted in June, they knew that their goodbyes were final. Althea packed up her car and headed home to Harlem.

In Harlem, she made it her business to see Sydney quickly, much as she dreaded it. She had to tell him that she'd applied to the Women's Army Corps. She knew that he'd be very upset, and he was. In Althea's words, "He almost had a fit." A few weeks later, Althea told him she'd passed the WAC physical. She could be called any day now. Sydney pleaded with her not to sacrifice all the years she had put into building her career. "Why would you do this?" he asked her. "You got a great future in front of you."

Althea felt grieved for him. But she shook her head. "If I was any good I'd be the champ now. But I'm just not good enough. I'm probably never going to be."

To please Sydney, Althea had put in her entry for the national championships. Once again, she was invited to play at Forest Hills, but "my mind wasn't on the tennis." As she'd expained to Sydney, she was sick of the position she was in.

I'm sick of having people support me, taking up collections for me, and buying me clothes and airplane tickets and every damn thing I eat or wear. I want to take care of myself.

She wasn't very upset when she lost in the third round at Forest Hills. This was her farewell performance, she thought. Soon, she would have a whole new career, in the U.S. Army.

But Althea Gibson wasn't going to serve in the U.S. Army. It was the U.S. State Department she would be serving, very soon. And her life, once again, was going to change.

■ ■ ■

It took Althea less than five seconds to make up her mind. When, at Forest Hills, an official of the USLTA came over to speak to her, she couldn't at first believe what she was hearing.

"The State Department," he said, "is thinking of sending a team of four American tennis players on a goodwill tour of Southeast Asia. And they specifically said they would like you to be on the team."

Althea's plans for a WAC career flew out the window. It couldn't compete with this chance. A chance to travel into a wider world. A chance for thrilling adventure. A chance to use her tennis, and for a purpose. She told the USLTA official, "I'd consider it a great honor." With her usual directness, she added: "Not only that, I'm dying for something interesting to do."

The other team members were white, and all top players. The men were Bob Perry and Ham Richardson. The woman was Karol Fageros. Karol was "one of the prettiest girls I've ever met; she's also one of the nicest," Althea wrote. "I couldn't think of anybody I'd rather spend a couple of months with."

She supposed that she herself was chosen, largely, because of her color. The tour's purpose was better relations with the countries it would visit—Thailand, Burma, Pakistan, India, Indonesia, and Malaysia. The people of those countries were aware of the bad racial situation in the United States. No doubt the State Department hoped the image of the United States would be improved by including an African-American player in the goodwill tour.

Indeed, in Althea's words, it turned out that she was "obviously the principal attraction of the group . . . played up everywhere we went." It was clear, too, that it was "because I was a Negro," and "we were traveling among dark-skinned peoples."

The Asians not only were particularly interested in me, they also were especially proud of me. The kids looked at me as I played, with awe and amazement.

If the State Department was using Althea to improve the image of the United States, she didn't feel exploited. She despised racism and had no wish to cover it up. She knew all too well that African Americans suffered daily cruelties, horrors, and indignities. In spite of this, she had a simple belief that she should serve her country. She hoped she could do that and serve her race as well.

Very early in the trip, a spirit of cooperation and fun developed among the four goodwill team members. Traveling together through strange lands, seeing new sights, sampling unfamiliar foods, they found much to talk and joke about. As often as not, their jokes were about themselves.

They had decided to save some of their expense money by doubling up on hotel rooms. Karol was reading on her twin bed one night while Althea washed her hair. Karol had never seen a black person's hair in its natural state. She shrieked when Althea came from the shower, her hair standing up straight on her head. Althea calmly began to set it with a heated hair-pressing iron. Karol yelled, "What are you *doing!*" afraid that Althea would burn herself. Althea comforted her, assuring her it would be all right. But Karol was worried until she'd fingered Althea's hair, after the pressing. "It looks pretty," she said.

As Althea wrote: "We were getting to know each other a whole lot better."

The differences between Althea's hair and Karol's were a minor matter. They were both impressed by greater differences between themselves and the women in many countries they visited. In Dacca, Pakistan (now Bangladesh), they saw almost no women among the crowds in the streets. This was because of "purdah," the Muslim custom of keeping women out of sight of anyone but their families. There were a few women at the tennis matches, but purdah seemed to keep most jailed in their homes. For a Western woman, it was unthinkable.

On the other hand, the girls and women Althea talked with in Pakistan had interests very much like those of Western young women. However, when they talked about going on dates to movies or parties, Althea found that they dated only the men they were engaged to marry. Also, their marriages had been arranged in their childhood by their parents. The women seemed to accept this.

Wherever the team went, they were lavishly entertained with food. Most of the dishes were new to them, and most were delicious. In Rangoon, Burma, Althea ate something that disagreed with her and was very sick. Each of the four was ill at least once on the tour. It gave them a new source of jokes and feelings of attachment.

Most hilarious to them was their journey on the Indian railway. They had not looked closely at their tickets. Not until the porter showed them how to let down the beds in their compartment did they see that the four of them would need to bunk in one room, an unusual and embarrassing situation in the 1950s. No other compartment was left on the train—and none of them wanted to spend the night standing in the corridor. They took turns changing into pajamas in the only rest room, down the corridor. Karol and Althea used the two lower bunks, Bob and Ham the upper. Throughout the tour, they laughed over this story—and years later, whenever one teammate met another.

Meanwhile, they went on delighting the crowds with their fast, powerful game of tennis. People also seemed charmed by their friendliness, their interest in the local sights, their high spirits. Everywhere they went, the young U.S. tennis players were, as one observer put it, "Topic A."

With all the attention, public approval, and private comradeship, Althea blossomed. Her game improved by leaps and bounds, growing stronger and more daring with each match. Her victories came to a peak in Burma, where she won the singles championship in the All-Asian Tennis Tournament.

Althea said later, of the State Department tour, "I've never done anything more completely satisfying or rewarding." She was sad when it ended, in Colombo, Ceylon (now Sri Lanka), in mid-January, 1956. She and Karol wept when they parted. Althea was staying on for several months more. She had accepted invitations to play in a series of tournaments, in a great many places. Her tour included matches in Stockholm, Sweden; Cologne, Germany; Florence, Italy; Cairo and Alexandria, Egypt; and Lyon, Cannes, and Paris, France.

Although she dated a young man or two, including one she liked a lot, in Egypt, Althea felt lonely without her teammates. Even so, after eight months of international play, she was in outstanding form. She had run up a remarkable series of victories, winning sixteen out of eighteen international tournaments, starting with the All-Asian championship. Her crowning achievement was at the famed Stade Roland Garros in Paris, where she won the French singles championship. This contest ranked in worldwide importance only below the Wimbledon and Forest Hills competitions.

No black player before Althea had won a French national championship. More than that, Althea was the first black person to win a major singles title anywhere in the world.

Althea had no reason to regret her lightning decision to say no to the WACs in favor of an adventure into the wider world. In the spring of 1956, she felt ready to face "the big one" again. She headed for England, and Wimbledon.

CHAPTER 5

Fame

It had been five years since Althea Gibson first played at Wimbledon. She had lost then, and her tennis career had begun a downward slide.

A lot had happened lately to turn things around. When she headed for Wimbledon the second time, in 1956, London bookmakers rated Althea Gibson the 2-1 favorite to win. After all, now she was the champion of France and winner of sixteen international championships.

No female player had ever played so many tournaments in a row—and no wonder! It was a huge strain on body and spirit. Even Althea—"no delicate flower"—was starting to feel tired. But that didn't make her a bit less eager to tear up the courts. When she reached England, she competed in the warmup matches that came in the weeks before Wimbledon. One of these was with Shirley Fry, another outstanding American player. Althea fought a tough, 100-minute match before she beat Shirley 6–3, 6–8, 7–5.

Then she went on to "the big one" at Wimbledon. As in 1951, she made it to the quarterfinals. There, she faced Shirley Fry again. Althea had every cause to feel confident. Her position in world tennis was far higher than it had been in 1951. She'd beaten Shirley only a few weeks earlier. Yet, with all that, at Wimbledon 1956, Althea Gibson went down to defeat 6–4, 3–6, 4–6.

What had happened? Even Shirley was puzzled. She declared, "I should not have won. Althea played so wonderfully." It seemed to Shirley that in the last set Althea "got scared" and played hesitantly. She concluded, "Nerves, I guess."

Some journalists agreed. And a number thought that there was a very good reason for Althea's "nerves." It was an "anti-Gibson atmosphere" that could be sensed throughout the crowd. As one writer put it, "It's part of my job to smell atmosphere," and "I didn't like the smell."

> I accuse the Wimbledon crowd of showing bias against Miss Gibson. I say it was this bias that helped rob Miss Gibson of a quarter-final victory . . . which, early in the match, looked coolly and comfortably hers. It wasn't anything that was whispered. It wasn't anything that was shouted. . . . It was just an atmosphere, tight-lipped, cold.

Another wrote:

> To pretend that Miss Gibson is just another player is to bilk the truth. She is the first colored player ever to invade a game that is riddled with snobbery. . . . Althea wants to be regarded as just another competitor, but it was very noticeable that . . . the crowd . . . did not applaud the Gibson girl. . . . The color bar dies hard in any sport.

Althea herself, as noted by reporters, remained "calm, uncomplaining." She'd been aware of the lack of friendliness in the white, British audience. Coming after the warm welcome she'd recently received, in countries where the crowds were mainly people of color, it had been a shock. Yet it had never been Althea's way to blame anyone or anything for her defeats. In the old days, she might have socked someone for insulting her. Even then, she wouldn't use the insult as an excuse for failure.

This trait of Althea's was a source of strength—and very soon, she needed it once more. For at Forest Hills in September, she faced Shirley Fry again in the finals. At Wimbledon, after she'd defeated Althea, Shirley had gone all the way to the top and was now world champion. On her part, in the matches leading to the finals, Althea so far hadn't lost a single set. But she lost to Shirley.

Althea was disappointed—but she wasn't crushed: "I was a long way from wanting to hang up my racket." She knew that she had played well, that she could play now on equal terms with the best in the world. When she congratulated Shirley, she meant it.

She and Shirley admired each other, as champions often do. So they were both pleased when, a while later, the Australian Lawn Tennis Association invited the two of them to tour the country. They were to play in all the major Australian tournaments and do some exhibition matches.

Althea and Shirley were well-matched. In their exhibitions, each beat the other many times, all across Australia. Each also won two of the four important championships they played. The Australian press raved about them, and the people treated them royally. "We really loved the country," said Althea.

Shirley fell in love with more than the country. In Sydney, she had a whirlwind romance with a U.S. businessman who worked in Australia. When he proposed marriage, Shirley accepted. Thus, she and Althea parted at the end of the tour. With some Asian tournaments still ahead to play, Althea was unable to stay for the wedding.

In Singapore, where Althea had a stopover, she was invited to play some golf. "I hadn't had a golf club in my hands for a long time," Althea wrote, but "of course I did my best to show off how well I could play." Her hosts were impressed.

> **They said I was a natural-born golfer. I didn't bother to tell them that I'm also a natural-born basketball player, baseball player, football player, bowler, boxer, and that I shoot a pretty fair game of pool, too. I didn't want them to think I was a tomboy.**

Clearly, Althea had regained every ounce of her high spirits. Her spirits soared still higher after she successfully defended the All-Asian championship she'd won the year before. She joked: "Maybe I couldn't win Wimbledon or Forest Hills, but I sure was hell on wheels in the Far East."

In fact, Althea was just joking. She still intended to win *both* Wimbledon *and* Forest Hills.

That was exactly what she set out to do in 1957.

■ ■ ■

"Don't get over-eager and rush the net," said Sydney. Buddy Walker put in, "Be sure you get plenty of rest this time."

Althea laughed. "Okay!" Her coach and the old leader of her play street were fussing over her like two mother hens, she thought. They were all in Sydney's car, on their way to the airport where Althea would take off for England—and Wimbledon 1957.

In contrast to her two previous Wimbledon tours, this year the USLTA was paying Althea's round-trip air fare and expenses. She was one of its world-class champions now. Even so, the USLTA didn't allow any of its stars a generous sum. Therefore, Edna Mae Robinson—who was part of the send-off party at the airport—slipped Althea twenty dollars as they kissed goodbye. Edna Mae and Sugar Ray, although not much older than Althea, were mother-hennish in their own way.

Althea's plane was met on the other side of the ocean by another friend, the British tennis player Angela Buxton. In the past, Angela and Althea had been singles opponents as well as doubles partners. In fact, the year before—when Althea had failed to win the Wimbledon singles—she and Angela had victoriously carried off the Wimbledon doubles crown together. Now, with Angela's boyfriend and Althea's bags, they jammed into Angela's tiny car. They drove to Angela's London flat, where Althea was to be her guest.

Angela hurried off to her job at a sporting goods store, while Althea left for her first warmup match. She planned to play in only three. She didn't want to make last year's error of wearing herself out before the main event. She won all three of these contests and arrived at Wimbledon "in top shape."

Althea towered over her first opponent, a five-feet-two Hungarian woman. Yet this match proved Althea's hardest, as she struggled for every point before winning 6–4, 6–4. She went on to play the semifinals against a young British wonder she'd heard about. This was sixteen-year-old Christine Truman, the darling of British tennis fans. Althea braced for another hostile crowd.

And that was what she got, at first. The fans made a lot of noise, clapping excitedly for Christine's every good shot. But—there weren't that many. The younger woman, far outclassed by Althea, soon wilted. The crowd grew quiet, spellbound against its will by the brilliance of Althea's game. By the time she clobbered Christine 6–1, 6–1, the audience was on its feet, cheering. She walked from the court amid a storm of applause.

The day of the Wimbledon final dawned bright and hot. Althea, who loved best to play in hot weather, felt wonderful. She was going to play on the famous Centre Court in front of the royal box. When she heard that the Queen of England was going to be there, she felt even better. She wasn't even very nervous as she made a graceful curtsy before Queen Elizabeth II.

Now Althea faced another American, Darlene Hard. A superb California player, Darlene had been a Wimbledon semifinalist in 1955. But Althea wasn't fazed. Her hopes were so high, she'd worked on a speech to give that night at the Wimbledon Ball, in case she won. She saw, in this, the foolish behavior of the brash, young, overconfident Althea—and she was nearly thirty! But she couldn't help it. She *knew* that she was going to win.

She did. She won the first set in twenty-five minutes. Her furious, dazzling play went forward, as Darlene fumbled, looking wretched. In fifty minutes, Althea polished her off.

Shouting, "At last! At last!" Althea leaped to the net on her lithe, long legs. Racing around it, she grabbed Darlene's hand and warmly congratulated her on her playing. Then they both walked to the trophy table, to meet the Queen, who stepped toward them on a red carpet rolled from her box.

The Queen shook hands with Althea, congratulated her, and they exchanged some pleasant words. Althea said later that the Queen "had a wonderful speaking voice and she looked exactly as a queen ought to look, except more beautiful than you would expect any real-life queen to look." The Queen handed Althea the trophy, a gold tray engraved with the names of all previous Wimbledon champions. Then Darlene stepped up to accept her runner-up trophy and the Queen's congratulations.

Next came the swarm of newspaper photographers, followed by the television interview at the clubhouse. In Althea's dressing room was a heap of telegrams—from family, friends, and many more—from the Williston Industrial High School principal to the governor of New York. There wasn't time to read them all before hurrying to Angela's flat, where both of them dressed for the Wimbledon Ball.

So Althea gave her speech, in which nobody was left out of her thank-you's—Buddy, Sydney, the Cosmopolitan Club coach Fred Johnson, Dr. Eaton and Dr. Johnson, the Robinsons, many others. She thanked all her opponents, whose fine playing had commanded her own best efforts. Then, as the Queen and other members of the royal family looked on, she and the Wimbledon men's champion, Lew Hoad, led off the dancing. Afterward, everyone else joined in. Later in the evening, asked to sing, Althea did so, to much applause. She reflected:

> It seemed a long way from 143rd Street.
>
> Shaking hands with the Queen of England was a long way from being forced to sit in the colored section of the bus going into downtown Wilmington, North Carolina.
>
> Dancing with the Duke of Devonshire was a long way from not being allowed to bowl in Jefferson City, Missouri, because the white customers complained about it.

Perhaps best of all, wrote Althea, was her letter from the president of the United States, Dwight D. Eisenhower. He seemed to grasp some idea of the long, hard road she had traveled. "Millions of your fellow citizens," he wrote, "join with me in felicitations on your outstanding victory at Wimbledon. Recognizing the odds you faced, we have applauded your courage, persistence and application. . . . You met the challenge."

There was more to follow. When Althea returned to New York, she was met by more than the three friends who had seen her off. There was a crush of newspaper, radio, and television reporters, city officials, and fans, black and white.

There was her mother, who cried and laughed as Althea ran to her. In Harlem, her father waited, yelling joyfully out the window of the family apartment.

Mr. Gibson wasn't alone in welcoming Althea back to Harlem. Althea was deeply moved when she saw "all those people come out of their tired old apartment houses up and down 143rd Street to tell me how glad they were that one of the neighbors' children had gone out into the world and done something big." Remembering her childhood on these streets, she mentally compared bringing home the Wimbledon trophy with the days when the trophy she'd sneaked home was "a mushmelon I'd snitched."

The next day, thousands turned out for a ticker-tape parade given by the city of New York. Wearing a spray of orchids on her shoulder, Althea was driven in an open car to City Hall. There Mayor Robert Wagner presented her with the city's medal. News photos recorded the smiles of the mayor, Althea, and her parents. They next moved on to the famed Waldorf-Astoria Hotel for a luncheon party given in Althea's honor by the mayor.

Just as Althea ate up every crumb of the tasty luncheon at the Waldorf, she ate up every glad moment of celebration. Soon she had another honor, that of being chosen for the Wightman Cup tennis team. The Wightman Cup matches were played between teams of the top U.S. women and the top British women players. The year before, 1956, Althea had been denied this honor and, for once, she had admitted her anger. She'd been the number two woman player in the United States, and she'd deserved to be asked. But the Wightman Cup officials, she later wrote, "just looking for an excuse," had used her 1955 ranking of number eight "to justify passing me up."

However, she soon forgot her bitterness. When, in 1957, she put on the white blazer given to every member of the

Wightman Cup team, she felt very proud. It was a thrilling experience to be playing not "just for Althea Gibson," but for her country.

The only trouble now was that, because of Althea's unusually long frame, her white blazer didn't fit. Turning before the dressing room mirror, she said worriedly to her teammates, "I'd rather not seem like I'm too fussy, but don't you all think these sleeves are too short?" The women—including her old supporter Sarah Palfrey Cooke—burst into laughter as they agreed. They got the sleeves fixed, somehow. Then they went on to win for the United States—the twenty-first straight U.S. win since England's 1930 win.

Then it was time again for the U.S. national championships at Forest Hills. As luck would have it, Althea drew her friend Karol Fageros for the first-round match. Karol gave her a good fight, but Althea won, and romped on to the finals.

The morning of the finals, she felt keyed up, "with so much at stake." Above all else, she wanted to be the champion of the United States. She had breakfast with the vice president of the sporting goods company for which she now worked, doing promotion for its products. Then Sydney—who, to her pleasure, was to sit with all the dignitaries at the match—drove her to Forest Hills.

The player she met in the finals was Louise Brough. It was Louise who, with the help of a thunderstorm, had defeated Althea in her very first appearance at Forest Hills.

But that was seven years earlier. The Althea whom Louise met in 1957 was a champion who played—as one sports magazine put it—as though she were "serenely aware" of being "the star." And she went on playing like a star. She defeated Louise easily, 6–3, 6–2. The New York *Herald Tribune* commented the next day that "there never was any doubt of the result."

Althea Gibson did not take the result lightly. It was far more important to her than winning at Wimbledon. She wrote: "There is nothing quite like winning the championship of your own country. That's what counts the most with anybody."

It was Vice President Richard Nixon who handed Althea the trophy. She gave a brief acceptance speech. Then she stood in silence, dripping sweat, her head bowed. From the stands, applause burst forth. Wave after wave of it swept toward Althea, an unceasing roar. Newspapers reported that even the oldest officials present couldn't recall a tribute so long and warm.

"Nothing quite like it had ever happened to me before," Althea said, "and probably never will again."

CHAPTER 6

Choices

Many times, Althea Gibson had hardly enough money to pay the rent. Yet she could travel just about anywhere in the world she wanted to go. That was because, when she traveled to tennis contests, her expenses were paid by those who sponsored the contests. At home, spending had to come from her own pocket. In spite of all the honors she'd earned—as champion of the United States, Great Britain, France, Asia, Mexico, India—her pocket remained skimpy. Her honors were trophies—not cash she could spend.

Her housing and food were better when she traveled than anything Althea could afford at home. Besides, she loved to visit new places. Therefore, after her 1957 victories, she spent nearly a year on a tennis tour of South America and the Caribbean. She enjoyed it, then came home to be coached by Sydney for Wimbledon 1958. It was very important to win this tournament the second time around. As Althea wrote:

> **In sports, you . . . aren't considered a real champion until you have defended your title successfully. Winning it once can be a fluke; winning it twice proves that you are the best. I was passionately determined that there wasn't going to be any "one shot" tarnish on my Wimbledon championship.**

And there wasn't. The shine remained on her first golden trophy as she smashed her way to her second one. Playing against Britain's Angela Mortimer, Althea took the final match 8–6, 6–2. "It was a wonderful feeling to know that I was . . . clearly the champion, even in the minds of those who had chosen to doubt me." To top it off, for the third year in a row, she also won the women's doubles championship, with a Brazilian player.

Once again, Althea took from British royal hands the gold trophy. Once again she danced as queen of the Wimbledon Ball.

Then it was time to defend her U.S. championship at Forest Hills. There she easily won her way to the final match, once again to face the Californian Darlene Hard. It was Darlene she had defeated for the Wimbledon crown one year before. This time, Darlene took the first set. After that, playing brilliantly, Althea crushed her 6–1, 6–2.

So Althea was still the champion of the United States and of the whole world. As she stepped off the court, she was at the height of her career. Tennis fans expected her to remain in the top spot for years to come. While Althea was thirty-one, this was in the era before young teens competed in adult tournaments. Althea Gibson had beaten the best the world had to offer. There was no reason why she shouldn't go right on doing it.

Sportswriters and broadcasters had recently named Althea Outstanding Female Athlete of the Year. A flock of these experts now crowded about her at Forest Hills, eager to hear her words in this moment of triumph. What they heard Althea say was: "I wish to announce my retirement from the ranks of amateur tennis players."

The reporters were stunned into sudden silence. Then came a babble of questions. All amounted to one word: "*Why?*"

The answer, too, could be given in one word: money.

In 1958, Althea had reached every goal she had set herself in tennis. In the process, she'd made great gains in knowledge and experience. Yet, in terms of money, "I am still," she'd lately stated, "as poor as when I was picked off the back streets of Harlem." Like other amateur players, she received no pay for playing. Her only income was a small salary from the sporting goods company which employed her part-time. She lived in a dim little New York apartment, with sticks of furniture she'd picked up from the streets. She had many trophies, and the respect of many people—and she'd kept her self-respect. She prized all that. But she couldn't eat her trophies or her self-respect.

How, then, was she to make a decent living? Often, retired players taught tennis as paid professionals at private clubs. But Althea knew that the rich white members of these clubs didn't want to have anything to do with a black teacher— not even a famous player like Althea Gibson.

Besides that, Althea didn't want to settle for the salary of a club professional or the life such a salary could buy. In her autobiography, she openly said so. "I didn't want to be a teaching pro all my life," she wrote. "I wouldn't become a professional unless I saw a chance to make a lot of money."

Althea might live in a shabby place, but she'd tasted quite a different life. On tennis tours, she traveled in comfort. She stayed at the best hotels and ate whatever she wanted. She didn't see why she shouldn't live well all the time. She had worked hard, tirelessly. She felt she had the right to see some money come out of that hard work. Not just fame, but money.

Althea hadn't yet realized how much she prized her fame. For the moment, she hoped to find a career in which her fame might at least help her get ahead. She also hoped to find a career she loved as much as sport. She decided to try to make a career—and a good living—in music.

Actually, this idea had been in the back of her mind for some time. As a way of gaining experience, she'd grabbed every chance to sing in public. For a number of years she'd been taking voice lessons, working hard at improving, giving more time to this effort than Sydney wanted her to.

At first, it looked as if her effort would pay off. Following a 1958 debut at the Waldorf-Astoria, she was signed by Dot Records to make an album. Before its release, she was asked to appear on *The Ed Sullivan Show*, a well-known television program of the 1950s. With her throaty, low voice, glamour makeup, and a new hair style, she was a hit. Ed Sullivan invited her back.

Althea confessed that she wasn't sure whether she was being invited as a tennis star or as a singing personality. But of one thing she was soon certain: sales of her album were *not* good, and offers to sing elsewhere did not flood in. Still, she wasn't discouraged. She began to look into her chances in the movies.

If Althea had talked with any well-informed black person in the entertainment business, she might have grasped how few African Americans made a living at acting in those days—far fewer than in music. Still, she got off to a good start. She was cast in a small role in a movie with two top stars of the time—William Holden and immortal box office hero John Wayne. Through her agent, she signed a contract for a very high sum of money. The movies! It was like a dream come true. Maybe even if she'd had good advice, she wouldn't have paid any attention.

For her role in the 1959 movie *The Horse Soldiers*, Althea didn't wear glamour makeup, but a "mammy rag" around her head. That wasn't a surprise to her. At the time, blacks played few film parts other than as servants. She drew the line, however, at the "mammy talk" called for by the script, such as "yassuh" and "yassm." She said that she could be true to the part without using language that wasn't natural to her. Unlike many actors, she refused to say lines that, in her view, "reflected so negatively and distortedly the character of a colored woman."

As Althea often said, she was not a civil rights crusader. In this case, however, she "felt that my own dignity and the dignity of the American Negro were on the line." She was ready to give up her film part, along with her big salary. When the film's directors saw that she was serious, they cut the lines.

The movie did well, and Althea received good reviews. Although no more movie offers came her way, life remained full of possibility. About the time the film came out, she received an offer in a field of entertainment more familiar to her than acting. She was asked to play tennis as the opening act for the Harlem Globetrotters tour. The Globetrotters is an all-black team of professional basketball players, founded in the 1920s. Their dazzling play, combined with comedy, had made them wildly popular. Their manager thought an exhibition of fine tennis would bring in even larger crowds.

Althea loved the idea. With Sydney and her lawyer, she formed a business corporation, Gibson Enterprises. She signed on Karol Fageros as her touring partner. Beautiful Karol was also a powerful player. She and Althea were an instant success. Although it was wearing to play nearly every day in a different city, they enjoyed the chance to travel together again.

Above all, Althea was grateful to make a good income doing what she loved best to do. With her share of the fees rolling in, she was able to move into a better apartment. For the first time, at age thirty-three, she had her own bank account. In 1960, she made a down payment on a house in the suburbs for her parents. It made her happy when they were, at last, in a place where they could plant a garden and hear the birds.

Meanwhile, the Globetrotters tour went from one success to another. When a year had passed, Gibson Enterprises was asked to renew its contract. To the surprise of the Globetrotters' manager, Althea chose to turn the offer down.

Why on earth should she do that? Her share of the profits was bringing in more dollars than she'd ever dreamed of earning. She had warm feelings for the Globetrotters—"wonderful gentlemen, courteous, sympathetic, and fun-loving." She liked and trusted their manager. It was true that touring, in her words, "can get to be pretty draggy." But she also understood that nothing came without hard work—and she'd never been lazy.

It had dawned on Althea, however, that for all her hard work, a huge share of the tour's profits went to the Globetrotters company. She and her advisors believed that Gibson Enterprises could make better money with its own basketball-tennis team. Looking back on this decision later, she saw that it grew out of several factors—her lack of business experience, her old problem of "a swelled head," and, she admitted, greed.

It was the worst mistake Althea ever made. In spite of her fame, people who were basketball fans wanted to watch the great Globetrotters—not her group of good but unknown players. With the stands nearly empty, the tour was called off in three months.

Almost overnight, Althea was ruined. She hadn't a penny, and she was deep in debt.

Yet, her famous name was still worth money. Very soon, a new offer popped up. She was again asked to tour the country—this time as a goodwill ambassador for the Ward Baking Company. She would give talks on her career at school assemblies, charity events, and other large gatherings. She was also to appear on radio and television shows, and in poster ads. She started at a yearly salary that was high, for 1961—$25,000. "Of course, I had to plug my sponsor's product," Althea wrote, "but it wasn't as if they made me do full-blown commercials. Just a few mentions of the Ward Baking Company . . . were sufficient."

Althea was popular with audiences. Youngsters and adults alike seemed to find her talks inspiring. Usually she ended her appearances with a song, loudly applauded. Well pleased, Ward Baking Company renewed her contract at the end of a year. Holding a tennis racket and pictured with a healthy-looking child, Althea went on smiling from the baking company's ads.

But inside her, there was no smile, nor was there any song in her heart. She felt like a fool, a failure, and a has-been.

Everything worth living for, it seemed to me then, existed in the past; money, glory, prestige, popularity and publicity, love and friendship, all glowed with the yellowed luster of unpolished trophies.

Badly depressed, she took no interest in her travels now. In a new city, she did no sightseeing in her time off. She could not even rouse herself to go to a movie, or to read. She sat in her hotel room, staring at the walls. "Who am I?" she thought.

Althea kept her despair to herself, however, putting up a good front for public appearances. "I wasn't going to let my sponsor or my audience down, especially the young children. What kind of example would I be setting?"

Althea had long dreamed of setting up a sports academy for children. She wanted to help young people as she herself had been helped by her two doctors and others. Her academy would train struggling young people for sports. It would teach them the values of sportsmanship and physical and mental health. It would give them encouragement and hope. As she'd begun to earn a good income, Althea's dream had moved closer. But after the Gibson Enterprises failure, it lay in ruins. She had only one goal in life now, to pay off her debts. Her answer to "Who am I?" was: "A woman who owes $25,000."

It was better than no goal at all. Through what she called her "two gray years" of 1961 and 1962, she had, at least, the pleasure of making her debts shrink.

But that satisfaction, alone, could not have returned Althea Gibson to herself. She needed a goal more in keeping with her natural drives. Tired as she often was after a day of lecturing, she found herself longing for a different *kind* of tiredness. Her muscles "began twitching" with a need to be in real motion.

Althea carried a tennis racket on her travels, but that was mostly for show. In her mind, the racket stood for all she had lost. When she became restless, she didn't reach for her racket. She turned her energy loose, instead, on a golf ball.

Althea didn't think about a career in golf the moment she headed for a golf course. At first, she was trying to escape boredom. True, her ability had been praised whenever she'd played for the fun of it. "Althea has everything," one golf pro had said. "The swing, the hands, the touch, the temperament. . . . Give her a year of work and she could be the greatest."

As Althea began to swing a golf club, her athlete's spirit responded to her recharged body. The fresh air, the sun on her face, were like a tonic. Feeling the thrill of whacking the ball, she knew something had changed.

Slowly, the wooly gray mist in which she'd been wandering started to lift. She began to feel more like Althea Gibson—a fighter. *That* Althea relished obstacles. Sometimes she had even sought them out "for the pleasure of wrestling with them." While she wouldn't have chosen to lose all her money—in fact, she'd always been proud of having no debts—she didn't regret her years of hardship. She learned a great deal from them.

Mainly, she learned that she could survive—even against the enemy of her own despair. She also came to value friendship in a new way. In times of success, people had flocked to her, attracted by her celebrity. Their interest in her had melted away when misfortune came. Others had firmly stuck by her. They were more precious to her now than ever.

Among them was William Darben.

Nearly ten years before, Althea had turned down Will's proposal of marriage. Her refusal had not led to bitterness between them. They remained good friends, with ties through Will's family, which had long ago "adopted" Althea. Will's sister Rosemary, an ATA tennis player, was Althea's close friend. Will, who worked as a production expert for a large company, was still unmarried and a frequent visitor in the Darben home.

Will and Althea—as newspapers noted—dated regularly when Althea was in the East. They were never out of touch for long, and Will was particularly kind to Althea in her period of gloom. In her second autobiography, she wrote:

> **Although I didn't realize it fully for a long time, I was coming to depend on him. He was like a part of me, but not so much a limb you consciously use; he was more like a vital organ . . . which you usually take for granted.**

Will had loved Althea before she was a star, he had loved her during her fame, and he loved her now, when her luck was down. As she began to realize how dear he was to her, Althea's feelings toward him quickened. Noticing the change, Will spoke once more of marriage. She was close to saying yes, but . . .

She'd made so many choices lately, some of them very bad. She decided to put this one off—if Will would wait?

He would.

CHAPTER 7

A Different Course

Shifting the heavy bag on her shoulder, Althea strode toward the golf course. A reporter trotted beside her. A little out of breath, he asked, "Could you say something about your future plans for golf, Miss Gibson?"

"No particular plans," Althea answered.

"You've been on the links an awful lot recently," said the reporter.

"Oh, well," Althea said. She tried to sound offhand. "Anyone can come here. It's open to the public."

She knew better than he that the golf course was public. Few private golf clubs in the early 1960s accepted African Americans as members. They didn't welcome them as guests, either. So where would black Althea Gibson play golf, except on a public course?

That, however, wasn't what the reporter had asked her. She didn't want to be rude. Flashing her dazzling smile, she said, "I just play for fun. To relax, when I'm not at work."

The reporter didn't look satisfied. "A couple of years ago, you said you're not interested in playing pro tennis. Would you say a golfing career is out of the question for you?"

Althea chuckled. "Well—anything is possible!"

"May I quote you on that?" the reporter asked. Althea laughed again and said, "Sure."

They chatted pleasantly for a few more minutes. Then the reporter watched, as Althea teed off. While her swing was impressive, she could be pretty certain the reporter hadn't gotten enough material for a story. But at least she hadn't hurt his feelings. She didn't want any bad publicity.

At the moment, she didn't want any publicity at all. She just wanted to be left in peace, to work on her golf game. She'd told the reporter more or less the truth. She really *wasn't* sure about a golfing career. It depended on a lot of factors.

She was sure of one thing, however: she was going to try to become a first-class, professional golfer. The public didn't need to know that—even though her employers did. Before her contract was renewed, she'd told the company about her new goals. It didn't seem fair not to: Ward had hired her for her tennis fame. But the company hadn't let her go. She was good for business. Ward Baking Company renewed her contract—and even gave her extra time to practice golf.

She continued to pay off her debts, thankful to have a steady salary. For, in the two bleak years of 1961–1962, Althea wasn't at all sure she'd ever earn a living from professional golf. She wasn't even sure she'd get anywhere in amateur golf.

To begin with, her age might work against her. Althea knew that excellence takes time—and she was already in her mid-thirties. She could expect her reflexes to slow in the years ahead. Besides, her reflexes were trained for tennis, not golf. She'd played enough golf to know it would be hard to change that.

And then, there was her old, familiar foe: racism. Althea's race would have blocked her from membership in most private golf clubs, even if she'd had the money to join one. That led to the same catch she'd faced in tennis. How could she compete in championships played at clubs where black people weren't allowed? Private clubs could easily get around the new anti-discrimination laws the civil rights movement had brought about.

Because of all these hurdles, Althea didn't feel as encouraged about entering golf as she'd felt about tennis. Still, she'd faced a constant uphill fight in tennis. She'd gained confidence in her ability to tough it out. And the civil rights movement *had* made a difference—both in the world and in Althea. She knew that the law was on her side, now.

Her ideas about her own role in the changing racial scene began to shift somewhat, too—at least, judging by her public statements. As early as 1959, when she'd toured with the Globetrotters, Althea had spoken out to reporters against segregated seating in a Virginia arena. She was to say, in 1963, when she was still a newcomer in golf: "My hope is, I can bring more Negroes into the game." In 1965, her complaints of bias against black golfers, in the North as well as the South, got into sports headlines. By 1967, she told an interviewer, "If my being out here and playing golf can be of some stimulation to other young ladies of my race to play golf, then I feel I've made a contribution."

These statements suggest that she felt closer to the fight for integration than she had in earlier years. Later, she herself noted changes in her attitude since her earliest days as a public figure:

I was a competitor. I didn't much enjoy being a spokesman for anything. But since then I've changed. What I feel now is that if I played tennis I would be playing for myself and my people.

Most of these shifts in her viewpoint, however, were yet to come. In her "gray years" she simply struggled with her decision to pursue golf and her efforts to excel in it. If her attitudes were changing, she didn't seem to take notice.

But in the early 1960s, attitudes about racial matters were changing in many others. Not only were black people revolting against racial injustice. Well-intentioned white people were also moved to act. Among them was a man named Jerry Volpe.

Jerry Volpe was a professional golfer who taught at the Englewood Golf Club in New Jersey. He was also owner of the club. He thought that Althea was a "fabulous" golfer. "With practice," he said, "I don't see how she can miss. She'd give pro women's golf a terrific jolt. Upward, I mean."

Jerry did more than praise Althea. He made her an honorary member of the Englewood Golf Club. She became, she says, "the only Negro, man or woman," among the club's members at that time.

Jerry Volpe's move had important consequences for Althea. For one thing, she no longer had to pay fees at a public court. She could concentrate on her game "without that voice of guilt" inside, scolding her for putting money into a risk that might fail. Jerry also gave her tips on how to improve her game. Most important of all, Jerry's support gave Althea's confidence a needed boost. With new hope, she buckled down to the labor of turning herself into a first-class golfer.

How hard it was! True, with her keen sense of direction and her physical strength, she could drive a golf ball powerfully and accurately over long distances. On the other hand, she had to learn "to hold myself in" for the slower movements needed in the short shots. Althea wasn't the sort of person to hold herself in, no matter what she did. It "brought out all my impatience," she wrote. She was "astonished at the variety of oaths" she could swear, as she silently bawled herself out.

Golf was organized and run in a different way than the USLTA ran tennis. In women's golf, the governing body was the Ladies Professional Golf Association (LPGA). Its members and its board of directors were all professional golfers. It was they who made the rules and decisions. This was unlike the USLTA, whose board consisted of officers of private clubs.

All of this meant that private country clubs didn't have the last word about who would be allowed to play in golf tournaments and who wouldn't. Of course, if a private golf club wanted to keep someone from playing there, it could refuse to okay that person for a tournament. But the LPGA could then move its tournament to a different club, as a punishment.

So, if Althea had the LPGA behind her, it might protect her from the racism and snobbery of the private clubs. Althea therefore wanted very badly to become an LPGA member.

Althea thought the LPGA rules for membership were fair. You needed to finish in the top 80 percent in three out of four LPGA tournaments in a row. These tournaments were called "open." Any amateur golfer could enter them by paying a fee of $50 to $100.

Once you got into the LPGA, you were classed as a professional. Althea faced the fact that the LPGA had no black members. But neither had the Englewood Golf Club, until Althea. The main thing, Althea figured, was playing well enough to qualify. She set 1964 as her target for LPGA membership.

In 1963 Altha played only a few tournaments. She didn't do very well in them. Her average of 84.5 strokes for 18 holes compared poorly with players whose average wasn't above 74 strokes.

With painstaking effort, she brought her average down to 77.5 in her target year of 1964. It was a great leap ahead. She observed that her total 1964 winnings of $561.50 looked "silly," compared to the $29,800 won by the top player. But she hoped to earn much more than that, herself, as her skills grew.

Meanwhile, she had reasons to feel happy. Her skills *were* improving. Besides that, the white LPGA players had welcomed her competition warmly. The same had been true of tennis players, but Althea never knew quite what to expect. She'd trained herself to meet hurts and insults with dignity.

That training came in handy very soon.

Althea finished in the top 80 percent in two tournaments running. She was overjoyed. Now she needed to do it again, in just one more contest—and she'd have her LPGA card.

On the bright day of that tournament, Althea whistled a tune as she ran up the clubhouse steps. At the door she met a white man wearing the clubhouse badge. "Hi," said Althea.

The man did not return her greeting or her smile. He said, "I'm afraid you can't come in here."

"Oh?" Althea was puzzled. "Why not?" she asked. As the man didn't move, she added: "I'm registered for today's LPGA tournament."

"I didn't say you can't play, I said you can't come in."

Althea still looked puzzled. "Where do players stow their things?" She glanced around. "Where do I shower?"

The man shrugged. "Couldn't say," he answered.

Althea now grasped his meaning. She remained calm. She had weathered worse. And, these days, with the civil rights movement in the news, reporters were very alert to such incidents. They would find out, Althea knew, and make a fuss about it. The bad publicity would hurt the club more than the club could hurt her.

Althea strode back to her car. She opened the door—but she didn't drive away. She threw in her purse, grabbed her golf bag, and locked the door. Then she walked around the clubhouse and out onto the green.

It was on this day that Althea played one of the best of her early golf tournaments. Finishing ahead of almost half the other players, she won her LPGA card. With relish, she recorded: "Unshowered I may have been when I left that place, but I was so enthralled with my triumph that I just didn't care a hang."

The following year, the LPGA moved the tournament from that club to another one in the same city. Althea never discovered whether or not it was because the club had treated her badly. The year after that, in a different city, she was again refused the use of a club's facilities. This time, rather than accept such conditions, she passed up the tournament. But as a full-fledged member, she brought her complaint to the LPGA. She observed later that the tournament wasn't held in that city after her complaint.

In this case, also, Althea couldn't be sure the city was struck off the LPGA tour because of her complaint. Soon, however, someone began to make noises about discrimination that were loud and clear. It was Leonard Wirtz, tournament director of the LPGA. He "finally boiled over" when told that a certain private club wouldn't allow Althea on its links for one of the LPGA's tournaments. Saying that the club's rules violated the LPGA's bylaws, he moved the contest to a public court. "Gallant Lenny Wirtz, five foot five, snatched Princess Althea, five ten and a half, from the teeth of the dragon," wrote Althea. She added that Lenny Wirtz "has my eternal gratitude for his moving display of courage."

Althea was, by now, giving so much time and energy to golf, little was left over for her job with Ward Baking Company. With regret on both sides, the company and Althea made a mutual decision to end their five-year relationship.

Althea still needed to support herself while she pursued her new career. It cost money to tour. She decided to borrow enough for expenses—$750 to $1000 a month. Her bank was willing to make the loan. Althea Gibson was star quality, considered worth the investment. Her golf was steadily improving, and her winnings slowly rising. She felt confident.

In fact, she felt confident enough to decide, near the end of 1965, to marry Will Darben. She wasn't broke, and she was making progress. There wasn't any reason to suspect that Will felt sorry for her, as there might have been the last time he'd proposed to her. Nor did it bother her for Will to be the main provider. She didn't need to prove she could make a living. She hoped that in a year or two, she'd make much more than that.

Meanwhile, marriage was a new and happy experience. Althea wanted her own home—that is, one with this particular man in it. Will and Althea had more in common than their long friendship. For example, they shared an interest in music. Althea had already known that Will played the piano. Now she discovered, with delight, that he composed songs, too. Their evenings at home were often spent at the piano, "making music, literally."

Will didn't go with Althea on her tours. His position at the Bendix Company got in the way of that. It was just as well with Althea. She found herself childishly nervous when she knew "my *husband*" was watching. They kept in regular touch by phone. Althea looked forward to coming home to his warm interest in her victories—and his understanding in the face of her defeats.

After her marriage, Althea's game shot ahead faster. In 1966, her average dropped to 74, and her winnings rose to $3,221.50. She broke the course record at the Pleasant Valley Country Club in Sutton, Massachusettes, scoring a 68. Newspapers charted her climb, while the bank gladly continued her loan.

Althea ended her second autobiography, published in 1968, on a note of high hope. But there was also a shade of caution. "We constantly tread the borders of discouragement," she wrote, "and the devil perpetually whispers 'Why don't you give up?'"

Althea Gibson wasn't ready to give up her ambitions for a career in golf as brilliant as the one she'd had in tennis. In truth, her playing showed flashes of brilliance. Even so, her game wasn't dependable. A smashingly impressive round was often followed by a weak one.

She went on working doggedly. But after 1967, she was never among the top ten players at season's end. She spent no money on "furs, pheasant under glass, or flashy jewelry," only on basics. Nevertheless, no matter how strict her budget, her golf earnings didn't keep pace with her expenses. After seven years on the professional golf tour, she was thousands of dollars in debt.

Althea couldn't afford to settle for being a middle-level player. Even if she'd had the money, her pride wouldn't let her. At the end of 1970, she called it quits.

In her 1968 autobiography, Althea wrote of taking heart in the thought that "The noblest and humblest stand equal under the banner that declares . . . WE TRIED." It was a modest way to describe her own accomplishments. She had shown both courage and grace in her stubborn attempt to overcome obstacles in the path of her goal. And she had again opened the way for African Americans and others of color—this time, in golf.

She could see that for herself, now, in a light that she hadn't seen her achievements in tennis. Like many touched by the civil rights movement, she had grown into a new understanding of the ways her personal struggle related to the struggles of others. It was a realization that would stay with her in her future in the world of sport.

For she still had a future in the world of sport.

CHAPTER 8

Passing It On

"Nice one!" Althea shouted, as she returned her student's serve. The young man's freckled face split into a wide grin. "Thanks!" he shouted. He slammed the ball back over the net.

They continued to practice for fifteen minutes, before Althea glanced at her watch. "Time's up, I'm afraid," she said.

"Okay by me," her student said. "I'm *bushed*."

Althea laughed. "Sure, but you're really coming along."

She waved to her next student, a pretty, gray-haired white woman coming from the clubhouse. Althea wiped her face with a towel, then took up her racket from the bench.

It felt good to have a racket in her hands again, daily. It also felt good to know that after this lesson, she could shower at the clubhouse. The club had hired her as its professional.

Much had changed since 1958, the year Althea retired as amateur tennis champion. At that time, she hadn't even bothered to look for a job as a pro at a private club with an all-white membership. She knew that those clubs hired black people only as maids and waiters. But in 1971, she didn't need to beat down any doors to get a teaching job at a private club. She found one quickly. It was at a club in New Jersey, where she and Will lived. The job paid very well, too.

Althea took some pride in knowing it was her determination that had opened the first doors to black players. However, she also knew that without the civil rights movement, the doors wouldn't have opened much further. She didn't feel like a hero.

Mostly, she didn't think about such matters at all. She was happy to be making good money doing something she loved to do. She still loved golf, and hadn't given it up completely. She played a few rounds once in a while. But her main effort went into polishing up her tennis skills. She wanted to compete again in tennis, this time as a professional. She hadn't played much professional tennis after the Globetrotters tour.

She had other ambitions, too. She paid off her debts and began saving money. In two years she had saved enough to invest in an indoor tennis club. When the club opened, it was described as "beautiful" in one sports column of the time. Althea's name was a big draw, and the club did well.

Althea's spirits soared. She felt ready to take on the world—well, at least, ready to compete in professional tennis. There was prize money to be made there now, as in golf. As in golf, too, the same tournaments had become "open" to both amateurs and professionals. Therefore, it was to the U.S. Open—as the national championships were now called—at Forest Hills, scene of her past tennis triumphs, that Althea applied.

At that point, she was informed that in order to qualify for the tournament, she'd have to play in some preliminary rounds. The former world champ was stunned. She was aware that ordinary players were required to prove their ability in qualifying matches. But was Althea Gibson expected to compete with unknown young players to show that *she* could perform? It had been one thing to start at the bottom in golf. Tennis was another matter! Saying only that she felt "turned off," she abandoned thoughts of competing in professional tennis. She continued to teach and to manage her tennis club.

But Althea's confidence had perhaps been shaken more than she knew. Certainly, after this incident, her life seemed to start falling apart. Her tennis club crashed financially. Her marriage of ten years headed for the rocks.

Althea fought against both defeats. "I'm not one to give up something I've started," she once told an interviewer. Her life offered plenty of proof. Nevertheless, by 1975, her tennis club had shut down, and she was divorced.

Althea was nearing fifty—an age when the future didn't look as rosy as it once had. On the other hand, she had gathered strength in her forty-eight years—from failure as well as success. Now she picked up the pieces of her life and went on.

For a few months in 1975, she continued teaching at private clubs. Then she had an opportunity that excited her. She was asked to become the manager of the Department of Recreation of East Orange, New Jersey. The city was one with a large number of poor families, many of them black. If it wasn't quite Althea's old dream of her own tennis academy for children, it was close.

Althea had worked briefly in similar positions during her pro golfing career. She had taught youngsters, on weekends, at the Milburn Tennis Center, in New Jersey. Its manager said of her: "She has the patience of a saint, even with kids who have never held a racket." In 1970, she had been appointed a special sports consultant for the Essex County, New Jersey, Park Commission. In that post, she'd worked with schools to bring children into tennis, golf, and girls' basketball. She had felt particularly happy "to use the talents which God endowed me with to make a contribution to the lives of young people."

It was no wonder, then, that Althea soon became a hero in East Orange, especially of the children. These were, after all, her people—the poor, sometimes hungry, often angry people of the kind she had been herself. And some were people, like Althea, in whom hope never quite died. She wanted to give them something more than hope—a way to enrich and improve their lives, to make their bodies stronger and healthier.

She knew best how to do this through passing on her joy in the disciplined play of sports. Her job in East Orange gave her a chance to do just that. It wasn't long before she was "kicked upstairs" to a bigger job. In 1980, she became Recreation Director of the City of East Orange. She was hailed in her new post by a news story that began: "There will never be another Althea Gibson. To meet with and talk with this woman is to learn a little bit about what it takes to be a champion."

Althea also served for a number of years as New Jersey State Athletic Commissioner. She was appointed in 1975, the same year she began her job in East Orange. After that, she regularly held positions on New Jersey sports bodies, sometimes paid, sometimes as a volunteer. She was kept busy visiting schools and senior centers, lecturing on fitness, and holding tennis clinics.

In spite of her crowded days, Althea didn't tire—and neither did her spirit of competition. In 1990, the magazine *Sports Illustrated* reported that "63-year-old former tennis great Althea Gibson . . . is attempting a comeback on the links." The reporter called her chances of success "a long shot at best." But, he added, "it would be hard to find anybody who isn't pulling for her."

It was a probably a fair statement. As it turned out, Althea's "long shot" didn't succeed. But no one thought worse of her for trying. People in and out of the sports world, including some who know her only as a legend, continued to admire Althea Gibson.

Years before, Sugar Ray Robinson had instantly admired tall, brash young Althea for her spunk. At that time she was,

by her own report, a street-tough, a loud-mouth, and hadn't
learned the first thing about manners. While the bad manners left, the spunk stayed. It went on attracting people, as
did Althea's willingness to work hard, her honesty, and her
sense of humor. With all that, she was quite aware of her
faults—such as her "swell-headedness." If her awareness
didn't enable her to correct all her faults, at least it made her
more tolerant of the shortcomings of others.

Althea's attractive character and her talents had carried her
far. In 1971, her achievements were recognized with her in-
duction into the International Sportsman Hall of Fame. Even
so, she had been denied certain rewards merely because of
the color of her skin. That kind of discrimination eased for
many African Americans during the 1960s and 1970s. But as
the 1990s began, the partly successful struggle for racial
equality had lost a lot of ground. Under increasing attack,
many of the hard-won gains in employment and education
had been chipped away. As the country's highest leaders, even
its presidents, looked on indifferently, an ugly tide of intol-
erance spread wider.

In 1991, in that darkening climate, Althea Gibson was the
recipient of the Theodore Roosevelt Award. It is the highest honor given by the National Collegiate Athletic Association. Althea was the first woman to receive the award in its
eighty-five-year history. The "Teddy" is given annually to a
person "for whom competitive athletics in college and attention to physical well-being thereafter have been important factors in a distinguished career of national significance
and achievement."

A newspaper account spoke of Althea's prominence "in
the fields of sports and fitness, beginning with collegiate
varsity honors in basketball and tennis." Althea knew that
without "my two doctors," she wouldn't have dreamed of
going to college, at all.

Since then, other black tennis players have found it easier to fulfill their dreams. The great Arthur Ashe began his rise to world stardom ten years after Althea's retirement. Beyond the grace of his playing, Ashe's generosity and beauty of character have outlasted his early death. In the world's esteem, no male tennis player, white or black, has filled his shoes.

No black American female player has filled Althea Gibson's shoes, either. They are not easy to fill. At her retirement, in 1958, she had twice won the U.S. and All-England championships, as well as the French singles title, and other international titles besides. In her brief career as a world champion, she had engraved a lasting place for herself in sports history. At the same time, it can be noted that the number of outstanding black female players has increased. Among the top women players since Althea's era have been Zina Garrison Jackson and Lori McNeil, both African Americans. Coming up fast behind them is young black player Chanda Rubin and, younger still, six-foot Venus Williams.

Althea maintains an intense interest in tennis. She has promoted the welfare of the sport in general and the progress of young black players in particular. Among other things, she has been active in the black American Tennis Association, the same organization that first pushed her forward.

Like all tennis players and fans, Althea follows the annual Wimbledon contests eagerly. She took a keen satisfaction in Zina Garrison's triumph in reaching the All-England women's singles final, in 1990. Although Zina then lost to Martina Navratilova, she was the first African-American woman to reach a Wimbledon singles final in the thirty-two years since Althea's second All-England Championship.

Althea paid special attention to the Wimbledon games in 1991, held a few months after Alice Marble's death. National Public Radio broadcast a program honoring the great star's memory. Alice Marble had shaped women's tennis sixty years earlier, said the commenter. She had changed it to a "power" game, of a kind played only by men—until Alice. Further, she had taken an important stand on civil rights. No one knew any of that better than Althea Gibson, whose memories of Alice Marble were shared with the listening audience.

"My story," said Althea, "is an example of how much Miss Marble has done for fair play in sports." She cast her mind back to Alice Marble's public letter of 1950, which had protested the biased practices that kept Althea out of the major tournaments. Alice's letter had changed that, opening the doors through which Althea charged.

Perhaps most important of all, to always-proud Althea, was that Alice Marble had taken her stand "because of my talent, not because of my color." When asked, "What was it Miss Marble said to you?" before the start of that first tournament at Forest Hills, Althea repeated Alice's message:

"Have courage. Remember, you're just like all the rest of us."

It was all Althea had ever asked: to be recognized as a human being "like all the rest of us," to be given an equal chance to take it from there—wherever she could.

Alice Marble was one of the people who gave Althea Gibson that recognition and that chance. In so doing, she passed on the best of herself to others. Althea has continued to do the same.

She started with little but a passion for sport and a daring spirit. Over the course of the years, she faced disappointments and defeats, yet Althea Gibson went right on wanting "to be somebody."

She is.

ALTHEA GIBSON
(1927–)

Outline of Life Events

August 25, 1927. Born in Silver, South Carolina, oldest of five children.

1930. Sent by parents to New York City to live with an aunt. Driven by poverty as sharecroppers, family soon follows.

1939–41. By age twelve, excels at many sports and cuts school regularly to practice them; is also frequent runaway from home. Talent at paddle tennis noticed by leader of organized Harlem street games, who introduces her to tennis. Given junior membership at Harlem's black Cosmopolitan Club at age fourteen; coached by club's tennis professional. Drops out of high school.

1942–45. Inspired and influenced by seeing "man's game" of white star **Alice Marble.** Enters and wins her first singles tournament, the New York State Open Championship, sponsored by the all-black American Tennis Association (ATA). Loses in finals of ATA's national girls' championship, but wins in both **1944** and **1945.**

1945–46. Befriended and encouraged by rising African-American boxing champion Sugar Ray Robinson and his wife, Edna Mae. In **1946,** at eighteen, Althea gets to finals of

ATA's national women's championships. Loses, but impresses Drs. Hubert A. Eaton and Robert W. Johnson, two black physicians interested in promoting gifted African-American tennis players. Accepts offer to go to Wilmington, North Carolina, to live with Dr. Eaton and his family, work on her game, and attend high school. Spends summers in Lynchburg, Virginia, with Dr. Johnson's family, traveling with him and other black players to ATA tournaments.

1946–47. Disgusted by Southern-style racism and segregation in Wilmington, but makes rapid progress in studies at "colored" high school. Elected captain of girls' basketball team; plays saxophone in high school band; sings at black clubs with jazz combo. In summer of **1947,** wins first of ten straight ATA national championships.

1949. With a black player of Althea's proven ability, the ATA decides it's time to test the color barrier which has prevented African-American players from competing in tournaments controlled by the all-white U.S. Lawn Tennis Association (USLTA). Following talks between ATA and USLTA officials, Althea is accepted for USLTA Eastern Indoor Championships. Competing for first time as the only black in a "white" tennis event, does well, is invited by USLTA to play in its National Indoor Championships. Makes it to quarterfinals. Graduates tenth in her high school class, at age twenty-one. Accepts scholarship to all-black Florida A & M University, Tallahassee, Florida.

1950. Reaches finals of USLTA National Indoor Championships. The next step—competing in Eastern outdoor tournaments sponsored by USLTA member clubs—is denied because of her color. After angered **Alice Marble** writes open letter of protest, Althea is invited to these "white" outdoor tournaments, does well. USLTA invites her to U.S. national championships at Forest Hills—the first time an African American has been allowed to compete there. Comes close to stunning victory over three-time Wimbledon winner and recent national champion. USLTA officials impressed.

1951. Plays in Good Neighbor Tournament, Miami, Florida, first black invited to compete in otherwise all-white tournament in Deep South. Invited to play at Wimbledon, in All-England Championships, this time breaking a worldwide color barrier. Gets to quarterfinals before defeat.

1952–53. Invited to all major Eastern tournaments. In **1953,** seventh-ranking U.S. woman player. Graduates from Florida A & M, accepts job as physical education instructor at Lincoln University, black school in Jefferson City, Missouri.

1954–55. Fails to get beyond first round at Forest Hills. National ranking slips to thirteen. Black tennis teacher Sydney Llewellyn begins coaching her. She has love affair with unnamed U.S. Army captain. Dissatisfied with teaching career and seeking a more lucrative job, considers joining Women's Army Corps (WAC).

1955–56. Travels throughout Southeast Asia on U.S. State Department-sponsored goodwill tennis tour with top-flight team. Warmly received in Asian countries, she recovers confidence and power, wins many victories. Competes in tournaments throughout Europe, winning sixteen out of eighteen international tournaments. Wins French singles championship, first black player to win a major singles title anywhere in the world. Before hostile audience, loses at Wimbledon. Loses again at Forest Hills, to world champion

Shirley Fry. With Shirley, tours Australia, each winning two Australian championships.

1957. Wins singles and doubles, All-England Championships, Wimbledon. Chosen for Wightman Cup team, which wins against British Wightman team. Wins U.S. nationals at Forest Hills.

1958–63. Named Outstanding Female Athlete of the Year (for **1957**). Wins Wimbledon singles and doubles again. Wins U.S. nationals again. At peak of career, retires from amateur tennis because of money needs. Publishes autobiography, **1958.** Brief singing and movie careers. Big success in exhibition tennis as part of Harlem Globetrotters tour, but ruined financially in similar independent venture. Works as celebrity promoter for Ward Baking Company (to **1965**). Hones golfing skills, although barred from private "white" golf clubs. White owner of Englewood Golf Club, New Jersey, gives her honorary membership.

1964. Qualifies for membership in previously segregated Ladies Professional Golf Association (LPGA), opening the way for black players to compete in professional golf.

1965–70. Marries longtime friend Will Darben, **1965.** Breaks course record at Pleasant Valley Country Club, Sutton, Massachusettes, **1966,** scoring a 68. Golf game powerful but uneven; not among top ten after **1967.** Publishes second autobiography **1968.** Leaves professional golf at end of **1970.** Appointed a special consultant to Essex County, New Jersey, Park Commission, she works to bring children into tennis, golf, girls' basketball.

1971–73. Inducted into International Sportsman Hall of

Fame, **1971.** Takes up career as professional tennis teacher at previously segregated New Jersey tennis club. Opens her own tennis club, which is at first successful, but fails in two years. Continues pro tennis teaching career.

1975–present. Divorced from Will Darben. Takes position as manager of Department of Recreation in East Orange, New Jersey, as director in **1980.** Appointed to New Jersey State Athletic Commission and other New Jersey sports bodies. Serves on New Jersey Governor's Council on Physical Fitness and Sports. Receives Theodore Roosevelt Award of the National Collegiate Athletic Association (NCAA), **1991,** first woman recipient in its eighty-five-year history.

The Game of Tennis

The following is a brief description of tournament tennis as it was played during the careers of Alice Marble and Althea Gibson. Some additional rules have been adopted since that time.

When one tennis player plays one other player, the matches are called *singles*. When two players play two other players, the matches are called *doubles*.

The game is played on a surface called a *court*. The court is the shape of a rectangle. It is divided across the middle by a *net* strung between two posts. The net is 3 feet high at its center and 3 1/2 feet high at the posts. On each side of the net, at a distance of 21 feet from it and running parallel to it, is the *service line*.

At each end of the court are the *baselines*. They are connected to each other by a pair of *sidelines*. The *inner sidelines* mark off the playing area for *singles*. The *outer sidelines* mark off the playing area for *doubles*. The playing area for *singles* is 78 feet long and 27 feet wide. The playing area for *doubles* is 78 feet long and 36 feet wide. The 4 1/2-foot wide strips between the *inner* and *outer sidelines* are called the *alleys*.

The area between the *service line* and the *baseline* is called the *back court*. The area between the *service line* and the *net* is called the *forecourt*. The forecourt is divided into two boxes called the *right service court* and the *left service court*.

In the middle of the *baseline* is the *center mark*. The *server* stands behind the *baseline*. The server must stand to the *right* of the center mark to hit the ball into the *left service court*, and to the *left* of the center mark to serve into the *right service court*, alternately. The server is allowed two tries. If neither try succeeds, the server loses the point, and moves to try again. Once the serve goes in, the ball is in play. (See diagram on page 172.)

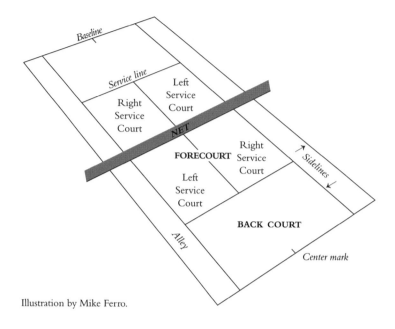

Illustration by Mike Ferro.

The *receiver* must return the ball before it bounces twice. In *singles*, the ball may land in any part of the court within its 78-foot length except the *alleys*, where it is counted as "out." In *doubles*, except for the serve, the ball is counted as "in" even if it lands in an alley.

Players continue to exchange shots until one of them fails to return the ball. The one who hits the last good shot wins the point. Play continues until one of the players gets enough points to win a game. The players exchange courts after every other game. This ensures that neither needs to look into the sun or hit against the wind throughout a match.

The *score* in a game is measured in *points*. The server's points are always called out first, even if their number is lower than the receiver's points. The word *love* means zero. (Yes, really!) For example, "love–30" means the server's score is zero, the receiver's score is thirty. The word *all* means a tie or equal score; for example, "30–all" means each side has thirty points.

The first *point* won in tennis is 15; second, 30; third, 40; and the fourth called simply "game." The first player to win four exchanges of shots wins a *game*, but if the score is tied at two or three points each, the player must win by a margin of two points. The first player to win six *games* wins a *set*, unless the score is tied at five games each. If that is the case, the player must win by a two-game margin. The score of a set may therefore be 7–5, 8–6, 9–7, 10–8, and so on. More often, a set ends when one player reaches six games, with a score of 6–0, 6–1, 6–2, 6–3, or 6–4.

In women's tennis a *match* is the best two out of three sets, meaning that in *singles*, the first player to win two sets wins the match; in *doubles*, the first team to win two sets wins the match. If one player or team wins the first set, while the other player or team wins the second set, a third set decides the winner.

Glossary

All-England Tennis Championships: Held since 1877 at the All-England Club in Wimbledon, a suburb of London, and considered one of the most important international tennis contests.

amateur: An athlete who has never competed for payment or for a money prize. Before the 1960s, the top tennis players were amateurs. If they took payment, they were no longer allowed to compete in official tournaments. Only their travel could be paid for. They might also be given a small sum of money for expenses while on tour. See *professional, pro*, below.

court: See tennis court diagram, p. 172. Tennis courts may be indoors or outdoors. The surface of an indoor court is of wood or other hard materials. Outdoor surfaces may be cement, asphalt, clay, combined hard materials, or grass. The harder the surface, the higher and faster the ball bounces. To succeed, tournament players need to adapt their game to many different court surfaces. Originally, tennis was played on grass. Most of the important tournaments were still held on grass courts during the careers of Alice Marble and Althea Gibson.

default: Failure to participate in or complete a scheduled match.

Depression, Great Depression: A time, starting in 1929 and lasting through most of the 1930s, when businesses failed and millions of people were unemployed.

doubles: In tennis, game of four players, with two players to each of two teams. See *mixed doubles*, below.

dowager queen: The widow of a king.

Eastern grip: A way of gripping the racket handle that is best for dealing with the low bounce of the ball on the grass or clay surfaces of tennis courts common in the Eastern part of the United States.

final: The deciding match in a tennis tournament, when the winners of the preceding semifinal matches face one another.

Forest Hills: Neighborhood in Queens, a borough of New York City, where the West Side Tennis Club is located. It was formerly the site of the U.S. national championships. Since 1978, the contest has been held at Flushing Meadow, also in Queens.

golf course: Large outdoor grounds on which golf is played. A standard golf course has nine or eighteen holes, which are also called cups. The object of the game is to get a golf ball into these holes, one after another, with as few strokes of the golf club as possible.

green: In golf, the area of closely cropped grass surrounding each hole. Also called a putting green.

Hitler, Adolph: (See *Nazi party, Nazis,* below.)

lawn tennis: The game which today is known as tennis, originally played on a grass court, or lawn.

links: A golf course.

Louis, Joe: (Joseph Louis Barrow), 1914–81. African-American boxer, world heavyweight champion 1937–49.

mammy: Formerly, in the South, a term used by whites for a black woman working as a servant, often a children's nurse.

mammy rag: Kerchief tied about the head and worn by a *mammy.* The kerchief regularly appeared in pictures of a broadly smiling "Aunt Jemima," who came to stand as a derogatory comment on black women. African-American protest during the 1960s put an end to the popularity of the "Aunt Jemima" image.

match: See "The Game of Tennis," p. 171.

match point: The last point needed to win the match.

mixed doubles: A game in which each of two tennis teams is made up of one male and one female player.

Nazi party; Nazis: National Socialist German Workers Party. The party seized and held power in Germany (1933–1945) under the dictator *Adolph Hitler*. It promoted anti-Semitism, racism, and the belief that the German people were superior to all others.

Nazism: The ideas or methods of the Nazis.

professional, pro: An athlete paid for teaching or coaching, and/or one who competes in tournaments for payment or for a money prize. In contrast to the past, today's top tennis players are all professionals. They may win large amounts of money from cash prizes offered at the important tournaments and even more through endorsing various products. From the 1930s through the 1950s, there were also some pro tournaments, but with smaller prizes, and limited almost entirely to male players.

qualifying matches: Matches in which players must demonstrate their abilities in order to qualify for increasingly higher levels of tennis competition.

Robinson, Jackie: (Jack Roosevelt), 1919–72. First African American to break the color line in major league baseball, 1947, when he joined the Brooklyn Dodgers. Admired for both courage and talent, he was an outspoken champion of racial equality.

Robinson, "Sugar Ray": (Walker Smith), 1921–1989. African-American boxer, eight times world middleweight champion, 1951–60.

round: In golf, playing of the complete course. See *golf course*, above.

round(s): See "The Game of Tennis," p. 171. The completion of one of a series of matches in a tennis tournament. The more important a tournament, the more players compete in it, so that in a big tournament there may be several rounds before the final match determines the winner.

serve: In tennis, to put the ball into play.

smash: In tennis, to hit, with great force, a ball that is over the player's head, as the ball is falling.

Stade Roland Garros: Stadium where the French national tennis championship tournaments are played. Together with the United States, the English, and the Australian national championships, the French is one of the four foremost tennis tournaments in the world.

tee off: In golf, to strike the ball from a small peg in the ground, called a tee.

tournament: A contest in which a number of people compete. *Tournament tennis* refers to contests organized and regulated by an offical athletic body and recognized as the means by which players may move from one level of competition to another.

tuberculosis, TB: An infectious disease which may affect almost any tissue of the body, especially the lungs. If not treated, the disease can lead to ongoing ill health and death. Until the early 1900s, of all diseases, it was the leading cause of deaths worldwide. In Alice Marble's time, strict public health measures had controlled the spread of TB, but the illness was still much dreaded. It is treated today with antibiotics, but the main treatment was, and still is, rest, fresh air, and nourishing foods.

U.S. National Tennis Championships; the nationals: The yearly tournament to determine the U.S. national champions in singles and doubles. An international competition among the world's top amateur players in Marble and Gibson's time, it rivaled the *All-England Tennis Championships* (see above) in world prestige. It has evolved today into the *U.S. Open* (see below).

USLTA: United States Lawn Tennis Association. It made and enforced the rules governing the major U.S. tennis tournaments. The official body today is the United States Tennis Association.

U.S. Open: Formerly, *U.S. National Tennis Championships*, for amateurs only. Since 1968, the event has been open to both professionals and amateurs—thus, the name change to *open*.

volley: To hit the ball before it touches the ground.

Western grip: A way of gripping the racket handle that is best for dealing with the high bounce of a ball on the hard cement and asphalt surfaces of tennis courts common in the western part of the United States, particularly in California.

Wightman Cup: Trophy awarded for an annual seven-match competition between women of Britain and the United States.

World War II: At its start, September 1, 1939, it included Germany and Italy on one side, with England and France on the other. Before it ended, countries throughout Western and Eastern Europe, Asia, the Middle East, and Africa were involved. The United States entered on the side of England and France on December 8, 1941. The war ended with the surrender of Germany on May 8, 1945, and of Japan on August 14, 1945.